DETOUR TO
HEAVEN

One Man's True Journey

To Suzy,

By

Dale Reppert

Dale Reppert
Louann Reppert

And

Gina Reppert
Tristin Olsen

Odenheim Press

Copyright

© 2017 by Odenheim Press
PO Box 109, Kutztown, PA 19530

This is a work of nonfiction. Names, initials, and places have been
changed to protect privacy.

Printed in the United States of America
ISBN 978-0-9984139-1-4
ebook edition created 2017
ISBN 978-0-9984139-0-7

Library of Congress Control Number: 2016962738

Cover design by Vault Collective
Cover photography by Jacquelyn Kolosow Photography

Scripture marked KJV is taken from The Holy Bible, King James
Version. Cambridge Edition: 1769; King James Bible Online, 2017.
ww.kingjamesbibleonline.org
(Public Domain)

Dedication

This book is dedicated to all of those who lifted us up in prayer. Our family, loved ones, friends, church family, and so many of God's sons and daughters who we never met, yet they prayed diligently and forcefully for us. Thank you.

Table of Contents

Prologue
Tristin: My Father's Love

Growing up, I took my father's love for granted. I thought every dad tucked their girls in at night and then yelled silly love proclamations from the stairwell for half an hour. My sister and I would screech, "Love you, don't let the ladybugs bite!" And Dad would reply, "Love you, don't let the crocodiles bite!" I thought it was normal for a dad to give his children special gifts on the plane at the end of vacation so they would always remember it. I thought it was normal for a father to stay up with his asthmatic daughter, coughing away, while he spoke with the doctor and rubbed her back in worry. I thought it was normal for a father to go shopping for his preteen daughters; and return excitedly with the stylish outfits he chose. As a teenager, I thought it was normal for a dad to buy a special piece of jewelry every Christmas and say, "One day, you'll have someone to take my place."

I took my father's love for granted with the the knowledge that he would always be there, but one day a diagnosis changed everything.

Chapter One
Nine Out of Ten

Sheets clenched in my hands I beg for relief as the seconds come slower and the pain envelops me. Ten days ago I underwent brain surgery to correct a congenital malformation of my skull. I should be getting better by now. According to the doctor, I'm about halfway through my recovery, yet this morning I awoke to the most unbearably intense pain. Excruciating surges of agony radiate from the base of my neck up into my brain, involuntarily causing every muscle in my neck and shoulders to clench tightly and refuse to release.

For a few brief brave moments, I part my eyelids and take in my bedroom's familiar ambiance. The walls are still the color of a nearly ripened peach and the trim remains the same silky white, yet the palette I once found so soothing now holds no solace for my aching eyes. As the spring's afternoon sunlight peeks through my shuttered blinds, a flash of pain bears through my eyes as if the sun itself is trying to melt them from the inside out. It may not look like hell inside my warm and cozy bedroom, but it sure does feel like it.

As jumbled thoughts cartwheel through my brain, a slight commotion from behind the double doors catches my attention. Writhing in agony, I gingerly glance to my left to see Louann entering through the doorway. If it were possible, I would have smiled at the sight of my petite wife charging through the doors and leading a small army of people, all determined to help me. I quickly scan the faces of her entourage and recognize my good friend Al, accompanied by two paramedics and a policeman from our small township. The grave looks on their faces are enough to alarm me, but the sight of the gurney rolling in my direction bluntly exposes the severity of the situation.

The gurney's wheels creak over the hardwood floors as the searing pain begins to work its way down my spine inch by inch. Pain doesn't usually affect me like this; in fact, my ability to withstand pain has become one of my defining character traits. I like to joke that I can never rate my pain above a seven out of ten because I can always think of something that is more painful. In my mind, a "ten out of ten" on the pain scale has to be something extreme, like having to saw off one of my own limbs. I had planned a nine or a ten for something equally grotesque, but what I feel right now belittles every broken bone, torn ligament, and serious operation I have ever experienced. I have to go above a seven but desperately want to hold on to my ten. *I must be at least a nine though; I cannot imagine being in much more pain than this.*

I am trying to concentrate on the pain when Louann comes to my side and softly speaks, "Honey, I know you said you didn't want to go to the hospital, but I really think it's the best thing for you right now."

"Lou, I just really need something for the pain," I manage through gritted teeth. "I'm sure I'll be alright if I can get some stronger medicine."

Pairs of eyes stare down at me intently watching my every shiver and grimace. The policeman pulls Louann aside, and they speak in hushed tones while motioning in my direction. I try to make out what is being said around me, but the pounding in my head effectively mutes all conversation as the beating of my heart resonates violently in my ears. The paramedics flank my bed, slide a sheet beneath me, and transfer me to the gurney with a swift skillfulness that can only come from repeated practice. I am in good hands, yet despite their proficiency, I scream out in torment throughout the transfer and continue to moan even after they set me down. It doesn't matter how still I lie, there is no escape from the pain; even the slightest movement sends shockwaves coursing through my body. Desperate, I again plead for pain medicine to no reply. My face contorts into a grimace as four seatbelt-looking buckles are fastened over my body in an attempt to secure me to the gurney. The buckles are pulled tautly and dig into my already hypersensitive skin. Finally, the female paramedic addresses my entreaties, "Sir, we will be able to give you pain medicine as soon as we are in the ambulance." For the first time today, I let out a sigh, hopeful that relief might be nearing.

The gurney wheels me away from my modest bed and into the hallway, as Louann tries to clear a safe path for us through the laundry room. Each and every tile we roll over brings with it an excruciating earthquake of agony at the base of my skull.

"Honey, it's ok, you're almost there," Lou tries to console me. The paramedics wheel me through the side door, past the bewildered eyes of my oldest daughter Taryn, my middle daughter Tristin, and my friend Al. They stand watching in stunned silence.

"Alright, ready? One, two, three, lift!" The paramedics hoist the gurney up into the back of the ambulance and I feel Louann's fingers rest gently on my toes. She tries her best to reassure me that everything is going to be okay, but her cheeks begin to redden and her eyes fill with tears. I want so badly to console her, to tell her that I am fine, and that things are going to be okay, but there is little room for words in between my groans and wails.

We begin the half-hour journey to the hospital and I scream along with the siren, every bump and pothole like a knife directly piercing into my brain tissue. I appeal again to the female paramedic, "Please, I need something to stop this pain. You said I could have medicine when we got in the ambulance. I'm begging you."

She stares down at me, a bewildered look on her face, "Sir, you were already given a pretty solid dose of IV morphine. It should have kicked in by now so just hang in there, alright? We're only a few minutes away from the hospital. We'll get you more help there."

Chapter Two
What's a Chiari Anyway?

I couldn't believe that I was in the back of an ambulance. *How on earth did I get here?* Just a few short months ago I was going through my normal routine as Senior Vice President of Investments at Morgan Stanley. I had been with the company for over twenty-four years and was one of the lucky few who could say with certainty that I loved what I did for a living. I'd be lying if I said the job wasn't stressful. My partner and I were personally responsible for the management of over two-hundred and fifty million dollars in client assets. I had approximately one-thousand clients who entrusted me with the hard-earned money they had saved for their weddings, home purchases, retirements and college funds for their children. This was the money they wisely put aside to ensure security for their families should some unfortunate tragedy strike. The magnitude and responsibility of my job was not lost on me. I was aware that I held people's lives in my hands, and I worked very hard, never wanting to let my clients down. The days I put in were long and grueling, often stretching well into the evening hours. I missed dinner at home with Louann and my family more times than I'd like to admit, but I truly felt that I owed it to my clients to make their financial wellbeing my number one priority.

When I started having headaches, I didn't think too much of it. My days at work were hectic; I was doing many things at once and probably wasn't eating or sleeping as well as I should have been. When they became more frequent and longer lasting, Louann became concerned. "People get headaches," I reassured her when she'd badger me about needing to go see a doctor, "That's what ibuprofen is for." But no matter how many pills I took, the medicine didn't touch the pain. Episodes of double vision, nauseating vertigo, and numbness in my extremities followed but were so brief in nature that I tried not to worry about them. I'm not sure if it was out of denial or out of fear, but I repeatedly ignored and minimized my symptoms, shrugging them off as if they were trivial. One morning, I awoke on my office floor, unsure of what had happened or how long I had been lying there. Realizing that I must have passed out, I knew then, or finally admitted, that something was severely wrong.

Soon thereafter, at the age of forty-five, I was diagnosed with a Type I Chiari malformation. This, of course, sent me straight to Google as I had never heard of such a thing. This rare condition is congenital, meaning I'd likely had it since birth but had been lucky enough to avoid being symptomatic for the first forty-five years of my life. A Chiari malformation is a condition in which the bottom part of the brain herniates downward into the spinal canal. I was told to picture the base of my skull as a funnel. In a normal anatomical position, the brain inhabits the wide part of the funnel, and the spinal cord sits in the funnel's narrow stem. However, in my case, the bottom part of my brain was trying to force itself downward into the narrow stem of the funnel to go hang out with my spinal cord. Often, this happens because the skull itself is abnormally small or misshapen.

I awkwardly tried to make a joke to soften the blow of the diagnosis, "See Louann, I knew there had to be a downside to being this smart. My oversized brain doesn't fit inside my head anymore."

My wife glanced affectionately in my direction and without hesitation replied, "Are you sure it's not just your small misshapen skull?" "How much space does it take for a peanut?"

My neurosurgeon stifled a chuckle, but I couldn't help but laugh audibly at my loving wife. *Well played Louann, Well played.*

After a slew of neurological exams and imaging studies, it was determined that I would require surgery to repair the malformation of my skull. I obtained a second opinion in the hopes that surgery could be avoided, but unfortunately the second physician agreed that I didn't have much of a choice. If I were to delay or forgo a procedure, my symptoms would worsen and eventually cause irreversible damage to my brain.

The malformation is so troublesome because it causes an obstructive buildup of cerebrospinal fluid (CSF), which in turn leads to increased pressure on the sensitive tissues of the brain. This abnormal amount of pressure on the brain can cause a variety of symptoms, including but not limited to headaches, nausea, vertigo, double vision, muscle weakness, extremity numbness, and difficulty swallowing. The list of possible symptoms is endless, and the presentation can vary greatly from one patient to the next. The goal of the surgery is to decompress the cramped brain and to restore the natural flow of the CSF. There are minor variations in the surgical technique depending on the state of the patient and the preference of the surgeon, but the premise of the surgery is always the same: to create more room for the brain and relieve the pressure. Three separate procedures are often used to achieve this objective: a craniotomy in which a small window of bone is removed from the base of the skull, a laminectomy where portions of the first two cervical vertebrae are removed, and a duraplasty where a synthetic patch is sewn in to artificially expand the membrane surrounding the brain. The surgery that my physician was proposing would be a combination of all three of these procedures. If all went well, I would spend the first night after surgery in the intensive care unit (ICU) and then an additional two to three days in the hospital on a regular neurology floor. The doctors estimated my recovery at home would take approximately four weeks before I could return to work, but I was as determined and stubborn as they come, and planned to make it back in three.

My neurosurgeon wanted to schedule the surgery immediately, but I opted to push the procedure back a month because we were in the middle of tax season, and I couldn't possibly leave my clients without an adviser during the busiest part of the year. We scheduled the surgery for a Tuesday, a few days after Easter.

Chapter Three
Post-Op

The surgery to repair my misshapen skull was rather uneventful from my point of view; I fell asleep before any of the good stuff happened. The whole procedure lasted approximately four hours and when I awoke in a hazy fog, I already felt worlds better. The intense pressure that I had become accustomed to at the base of my skull was fully alleviated and I felt like an entirely different person. If I could have gotten out of bed, I would have wrapped Dr. Andrews in a giant bear hug, but having just had brain surgery, I mustered a simple thank you before drifting back into an opiate-induced slumber.

The next morning, I was somewhat surprised when I awoke to a crushing headache and stiff neck. I had expected some degree of pain during recovery but this seemed a tad bit excessive. My hands frantically rifled through my sheets in search of the call bell to ring my nurse. Upon her arrival, she administered some more pain medicine and assured me that she'd inform my doctor that I wasn't feeling well. After a few more hours of increasingly worsening symptoms, Dr. Andrews came down to my room to tell me that he believed I had developed something called chemical meningitis, which can be a rather common complication of the surgery. Chemical meningitis occurs when the meninges, or thin membranes that surround the brain, become inflamed due to the trauma of a surgical procedure rather than from an infectious source. There is no real treatment for chemical meningitis as the symptoms typically resolve as the inflammation subsides. I was prescribed a steroid called Prednisone to help decrease the inflammation and swelling that encompassed my brain. While the headaches persisted through Friday, they had abated just enough that my medical team felt that I was safe to be discharged home with close follow-up.

I thought my recovery would be easier with all the comforts of home, but my condition continued to be a tumultuous rollercoaster of ups and downs. Saturday morning, my daughter Taryn called my good friend Mike, who also happened to be the physician who delivered two of my three children. Mike stopped by the house to give me a once-over and apparently didn't like what he saw. Before I knew it, Mike was on the phone with my neurosurgeon. The two doctors exchanged pleasantries and then began discussing my condition, speaking in sophisticated medical jargon that far exceeded my level of comprehension; I had no idea what they were talking about. After getting off the phone with Dr. Mike, Dr. Andrews decided to bump up the dosage of my steroids as they didn't seem to be helping me as much as he had expected. The increased dosage of Prednisone actually seemed to work and I felt much better from Saturday evening until Wednesday. On Wednesday evening, now eight days post-surgery, my headaches returned with a vengeance, and Louann called Dr. Andrews' office. My steroid dosage was increased once more. By Friday, my incision began leaking a clear serous fluid, and its edges were dotted with small honey-colored pustules. My wife picked up some triple antibiotic ointment from the pharmacy to apply to the incision, and we phoned the office again. Dr. Andrews' assistant let us know that we were scheduled for a follow-up appointment in a few days on Monday, and they would re-assess my situation at that visit.

Sunday morning, I awoke feeling worse than I had felt all week. I barely slept the previous night and struggled to find relief despite hefty doses of steroids. My family later told me that I behaved completely out of character as I shuffled into the kitchen and gruffly barked out an order to my wife, "Louann, make me some eggs! Now!" This was odd for a few different reasons: First, I am a cereal guy and typically indulged in a big bowl of Cocoa Krispies for breakfast. Secondly, I'm not the type of person to ever take that tone with my wife. Also strange, I was donning an oversized pair of black sunglasses indoors to shield my eyes. I felt incredibly agitated and struggled mightily to keep my temper in check, a battle I lost when Tristin dropped a pen on the floor, and I exploded in anger at the sound it produced. I could tell everyone was walking on eggshells around me, scared that their every movement was going to set me off. *What was happening to me?* I ignored the eggs Louann dutifully set in front of me and instead asked for her to help me to the family room so I could lay down on the couch away from the everyday noises, lights, and activity of our household that had become unbearable.

The pain continued to escalate throughout the day so Louann called our neighbor Claudia, a retired nurse. She came down the block to our home, took one look at me, and insisted we call Dr.

Andrews immediately. Louann, feeling foolish, didn't want to bother Dr. Andrews again after having already spoken to him earlier that morning. He had told her that I still suffered from chemical meningitis and he'd take a look at me the next morning. At a loss, she helped guide me to the comfort of our bed, hoping I would be able to get some rest, but things only worsened from there. My pain intensified and I could no longer keep from moaning or yelling out in agony. I thrashed around in my bed for an hour and repeatedly refused Louann's pleas to let her call an ambulance. Finally, she phoned my friend Al.

Al was out mowing his lawn when his mower unexpectedly broke down and stalled. He ran inside to grab his toolbox when he heard his house phone ring and picked up to hear a terrified Louann on the other end of the line. Less than ten minutes later Al was by my side, having called 911, and an ambulance was dispatched to my home. I am grateful to this day that Al's lawnmower decided to stop working at the exact same moment that Louann called for help. I believe it was divine intervention. God wanted me to get to the hospital.

Chapter Four
An Overnight Observation

I finally felt the ambulance ease to a stop and was immediately wheeled into the emergency room, leaving my distressed wife out in the lobby to talk to the triage staff. Even with numerous doctors, nurses, and patients swirling around me, I could only focus on my own body. All of my senses were exponentially magnified; the fluorescent lights bore through me like a laser; and the everyday din of the emergency department felt like standing next to the amplifier at a heavy metal concert. I was fairly certain that at any moment my brain would explode out of my ears like an angry cartoon character. "Turn off those lights!" I shouted wildly to no one in particular. People began to stare, probably wondering what could possibly be wrong with the man being wheeled down the hall, sporting sunglasses indoors, and crying out to anyone who would listen.

As I reached my room, I frantically looked around trying to locate Louann. I felt frightened and wanted— *no, scratch that, I needed*— her next to me. After a few harrowing minutes, the curtain was pulled back and I caught a glimpse of her blonde hair as she made her way towards me. Coming in behind her was the emergency room physician. A man my age, the ER doc was notably calm and self-assured. To him, the scene in the ER wasn't frenzied or even the least bit out of the ordinary; it was just another Sunday. He asked us to give him a quick run-down of the events that occurred leading up to today; specifically, he asked about my sunglasses and how long I had been feeling the need to wear them. My wife gave a quick history, "Less than two weeks ago, Dale underwent surgery to repair a Type 1 Chiari malformation. We spoke with his neurosurgeon this morning and were told he likely has chemical meningitis, and the pain was normal and should improve. Only, it hasn't been—it's been worsening and now his incision looks red and is draining. The sunglass wearing started this morning; even the smallest amount of light seems to hurt his eyes. My husband typically tolerates pain pretty well; I've never seen him like this."

The doctor scribbled on a notepad that he pulled out of his jacket pocket, his eyebrows furrowed in thought. He turned his attention to me, "Mr. Reppert, I'd like to order up a few tests to get a better idea of what's going on. I'll put you on a morphine drip to help with the pain and we'll try to get to the bottom of this, okay? Once I get some results back, we can go from there."

Despite the opiate drip, I continued to writhe in pain, pulling sharply at my hair in a lame attempt to distract myself from the rhythmic thumping inside my skull. At first I wasn't sure if I was imagining it or not, but I saw Dr. Andrews at the foot of my bed. I guess the ER doctor must have consulted him, and he had come to see me. After a hasty hello and a quick physical exam, he reiterated the same instructions he had given Louann and I over the phone earlier that morning. He said they could keep me overnight on the neurology floor for precautionary purposes and pain control, but I'd likely be discharged after morning rounds. The emergency room physician deferred to the specialist as per protocol, and no further testing was carried out at that time. Upon Dr Andrews' orders, the nurses came in and prepped me for admission to the neurology floor.

Seeing Dr. Andrews provided some much needed reassurance for my family as well as for me. My wife, kids, and Al decided to head home around 11:00 p.m. that evening. As my children said their goodbyes, I found it was increasingly difficult to make out what they were saying, as if my brain was a step behind. It felt much like when I was watching TV and, for some reason, the picture was delayed and didn't quite sync up with the audio. I was still able to understand what the characters were saying, but it was more of a struggle to try and keep up. Only this wasn't a television show, this was happening in real time, and I couldn't shut it off or change the channel. My wife walked over to the side of my bed, sat down close to me, took my hand in hers and said, "I'll be back tomorrow, honey. Everything's going to be alright, try to get some rest. I love you."

I held her hand tightly, not really wanting to let her go, but concentrated through the pain enough to tell her not to worry, that I'd be okay, and that I loved her dearly. With that, I attempted to put on my bravest face and watched her leave through the curtain at the foot of my bed.

Chapter Five
Louann: Falling for Dale

I struggled leaving Dale behind as I headed back to the cozy rural home we planned to grow old in together. While I was somewhat comforted by Dr. Andrews' assurance that Dale would be coming home tomorrow, my heart hung heavy with concern as I recalled the amount of pain he was in when I left. *He certainly didn't look well enough to come home.* We had been through our fair share of adversity together throughout our twenty-three years of marriage, yet I'd never seen Dale look so vulnerable. Memories flooded my consciousness as I drove the quiet two-lane country road home.

I grew up in a very large family with a woefully small shoestring budget. My five sisters, two brothers, and I all shared an unfinished attic that felt like the tundra during the winter, the Sahara Desert in the summer, and Transylvania all year long thanks to all the bats that frequently visited. My father died of a heart attack when I was 11 years old. My mother eventually remarried and moved our family to a small farm in Kempton, Pennsylvania, where the population was only 200 people until we came along and bumped it up to 210. The move gave us a bit more space, but in a family of ten, it was still very easy to get lost in the shuffle. Being the sixth of eight children, I never really knew what it felt like to have the full attention of a loved one. That all changed when I met Dale.

I suffered from shyness and lacked confidence before I met my husband. We attended the same high school, but our groups of friends never really mingled. Dale was the perfect mix of jock, musician, and overall nice guy. Although I had my small group of friends, I would likely be considered a late bloomer in today's society. My braces and oversized glasses made me self-conscious, and I often was too shy to socialize outside of my tight-knit circle.

Dale and I wound up attending the same medium-sized university, where our paths eventually crossed. After weeks of making eye contact with him in the hallways between classes, we were formally introduced in the school library by a mutual friend. I was nineteen years-old, and Dale was twenty-one. A few days later, I was working the cash register at a local department store when I caught a glimpse of Dale's slender 6'1" frame heading in my direction. I was caught off guard and momentarily panicked and quickly had to talk myself down. *Play it cool Louann, play it cool.* I was somewhat surprised to see that Dale looked just about as nervous as I was. He leaned on the service desk, and his blue eyes sheepishly met mine; he dragged a hand through his dirty blonde hair as he tried to work up the courage to ask for my phone number. "Look Louann, I know this isn't the right place to ask you for a date but I was wondering if I could at least ask you for your phone number? That way I could go about asking you out properly. I apologize for showing up at your work like this, but I really didn't want to have to wait until school on Monday," he grinned hopefully and dug his hands into his pockets nervously awaiting my response. *How could I possibly say no to that?*

Sure enough, the next day he called to ask me on a proper date. He pulled up to our farm house in a well-kept ten year-old Mercury Cougar and took me to go see the movie "House Calls" starring Walter Matthau and Glenda Jackson. About halfway through the movie, he reached for my hand and I felt the hair on the back of my neck stand up. Admittedly, I can't recall much about the plot of the movie, but I will always remember the way I felt the first time his hand found mine. As he dropped me off that evening, I bristled with anticipation regarding the possibility of a goodnight kiss. While at my doorstep, I thanked him for the wonderful evening, and he remarked that the pleasure was all his. He sweetly and politely leaned forward to give me a small peck on the lips, both hands held nervously at his sides unsure of where to put them. Despite the innocence of it, there was an immediate spark of electricity between us. I remember watching him walk back to the Cougar and thinking to myself, *One day I'm going to marry this man.* As crazy and cliché as it sounds, I was only nineteen years-old at the time; but I had never been more sure of anything in my entire life.

My mind was jolted back to the present moment when I pulled into the driveway and caught a glimpse of my fourteen year-old son Tyler, through the front window. He was seated at the kitchen table helplessly staring off into the distance; he looked completely and utterly lost. I spent a few quiet minutes in the garage readying myself to face my youngest child. I needed to reassure him everything was going to be okay, even if I wasn't quite sure of it myself.

I wiped my tears, pasted a smile to my face, and made my way into the house.

Chapter Six
My Night of Hell

After Louann left, I found myself in a private room on the fifth floor of the hospital. The room was blanketed in darkness save for the sliver of light that snuck underneath the hallway door. Nurses and technicians popped in and out of my room, each one appearing to check a different pump, medicine, or vital sign. Desperately, I asked each person who came though my doorway whether it was time for my next dose of pain medicine. The nurse said thirty minutes. *Surely, it has been thirty minutes by now.*

Left alone, I continued to pull at my hair with both hands using the pain from my scalp to distract from the war that was raging inside my skull since I awoke early Sunday morning. It was now 1:00 a.m. on Monday and I was still trying to cope with this unrelenting agony. To survive, I had to break time down into more manageable blocks. I developed an odd ritual of sorts; I'd take ten big deep breaths and then clench my fists as hard as I could for five to ten seconds at a time. After I was done with that, I'd allow myself to tug on my hair for a couple seconds and then I'd repeat the whole process from the beginning. Each second became an exercise in surviving, a true test of my physical and mental conditioning for which I unfortunately felt wholly unprepared. A few days ago, I had been enjoying dinner at home with my family and now I was fighting tooth and nail just to keep my wits about me. *There was no way I was getting discharged tomorrow morning.*

Reppert, Dale	DOB: 03/13/1957	Neurology Service 5 East	MR #: MA006481920
OFFICIAL HOSPITAL RECORD— Nursing Notes:	0100 hours: Patient yelling and banging side rails in pain		Vital Signs: 198/89 BP 92 bpm HR 28 RR 98. 9 deg F temp
	0130 hours: Patient verbalizes severe neck spasms		

That night I experienced loneliness that I never knew possible; my room was a deserted island, my pain an unrelenting wave pummeling its shores. Every time I tried to think of my wife and children a crash of despair would bring me back to my current situation. I tried praying; I prayed for relief from the pain, and I prayed to see my wife's loving face in the morning. My faith was a blessing and knowing that God watched over me was an immense comfort. Despite knowing that He was with me in my suffering, I couldn't help questioning why I was allowed to experience such incessant agony.

Chapter Seven
Louann: Husband and Father

I couldn't recall the last time I slept without Dale next to me. Our bed felt so empty that I lined up pillows vertically in Dale's spot, hoping to trick my weary mind into believing that he was right there beside me. It didn't work.

A fitful night of sleep ensued, and I awoke with a start as the alarm blared through our bedroom with a resounding ring. I willed myself through our family's typical Monday morning routine in an attempt to bring a shred of normalcy back to our household. I made sure homework found its way into the correct backpacks and shuttled the kids out the door just in time to catch the school bus. As my bleary eyes lost sight of the yellow vehicle, I shifted my full focus back to the health and wellbeing of my devoted husband.

Heading back to the hospital Monday morning, I couldn't stop thinking about how much I despised the concept of "Visiting Hours." I hated having to "visit" my husband. It didn't feel right leaving him when he needed me the most. Throughout our marriage, Dale had always been by my side, supporting me through my darkest moments and reveling with me in life's great joys. The combination of both extremes had made our marriage such a strong and enduring bond. We truly appreciated the sunny moments because we had weathered our share of stormy ones together. Soon after Dale and I began dating, I received a phone call that my seventeen year-old brother, Ralph, had suddenly collapsed while at cross-country practice. Dale drove me to the hospital and held me tightly as I sobbed for hours on end after Ralph passed. The weeks and months that followed my younger brother's death were not easy; I suffered from waves of depression and struggled to cope with the unfairness of it all. I became angry with God, and my faith wavered. The stress of the tragedy could have easily wreaked havoc on a budding romantic relationship, but it somehow brought Dale and me closer together. I could tell early on that this man would stick with me through anything and that we were stronger together than we ever could be apart.

Luckily for Dale and me, the sunny moments far outweighed the stormy ones. In July of 1984, we were blessed and humbled by the experience of becoming first-time parents to a gorgeous baby girl, Taryn. She was our little firecracker, born on the Fourth of July and as independent as her birth date implied. From the start, Dale was a natural when it came to being a father. He was kind, caring, and extremely patient with our brand new addition. Taryn was adorable, but she was also very colicky. She cried incessantly for hours and hours to the point where her little face would scrunch up and turn beet-red as if she was about to stop breathing. As a new mom, this was pretty distressing, but the pediatrician assured us that Taryn was a healthy baby and this would just be a temporary phase. Despite working sixty-hour weeks himself, Dale would rush home to help care for Taryn and give me some much needed respite from the relentless screaming that permeated through our once peaceful home. He'd wrap our baby girl up in his arms and rock her gently back and forth, attempting to soothe her with soft words and delightfully hummed melodies.

We were blessed twice more with the births of Tristin and Tyler, each child entering the world two years after the one before. As in all families, with each child came more responsibility but also a multitude of new joys and experiences. Dale was the breadwinner and provided for us financially, working long hours to ensure we had everything we needed and more. What I remember most about Dale though wasn't the money he brought in, but the way he cared for our children. When Tristin was a toddler, she developed a nasty case of croup and had a horrible barky cough that we could not get under control no matter how hard we tried. As night fell, her breathing would become more labored and she would wheeze heavily. Oddly, the only thing that provided our sweet girl any relief was the cool air outside. I can still picture Dale standing out there for an hour at a time, holding Trissy snugly in a warm blanket, peeking through the back window and trying to watch TV. That was the kind of Dad he was, never complaining, happily doing what needed to be done for our children.

Before we had kids, Dale and I talked about what it would be like to be parents; how we would act, who would be the stern one, who would spoil them too much, and so on. One thing I always remember him saying is that he wanted to make sure our children didn't grow up in a dysfunctional environment like he did. His childhood was marred by household tension between his mother and father and everyone always felt like they were walking on eggshells. The atmosphere at the Reppert household was absolutely combustible; dishes were thrown, furniture was broken, people were screaming obscenities at one another — it was chaos. Dale once told me that he had to run three blocks up the street to get help from the minister after his mother knocked his dad out with a frying pan. He was ten years old; he didn't know who to call for help. As a result of the domestic dysfunction, Dale would try to stay outside of the house as much as possible, finding refuge in sports, music, and work. He's the most competitive person I've ever met and no matter what he did, whether it be basketball, saxophone, playing cards, or investing money, he had to be the best at it. To me, it always seemed like he was trying to earn his parents' recognition, to rise above the madness at home, but no matter what he did or what trophy he came home with, he was met with minimal recognition or praise. Dale knew his parents loved him and I'm sure they were proud of their son. I just wish they had taken the time to tell him that more often.

Dale made sure that things would be different when he had children of his own. He did little things that made each child feel special in their own way, bringing the girls flowers on Valentine's Day, taking Tristin and Taryn to see their favorite musicals, and letting Tyler beat up on him while playing video games or basketball. It showed them that he understood them as individuals and that he loved them for who they were. He created wonderful holiday traditions for our family and made it a point to be there for his children to support them at tennis matches, school plays, and graduations.

As I drive into the hospital again today, I can't help but pray that I find him better off than I left him last night.

Chapter Eight
Trying to Comply

The light of morning through my hospital room's window brought with it the hope of a new day. My nurse came to check on me, this time with the sun highlighting her face in a way I wasn't able to see last night; she was somewhere in her forties I would guess, right around my own age. "How are we doing this morning, Mr. Reppert? Any improvement from last night?"

"No," I grunted dejectedly.

"How would you rate the pain currently on a scale from one to ten?"

Without wavering, I once again replied, "Ten" and even that felt like I was understating it. I had never experienced this amount or type of pain before in my entire life: broken bones, a ruptured appendicitis, a thoracotomy procedure…nothing compared.

The nurse wrapped my right arm snugly in a blood pressure cuff and gently tapped the screen of my monitor as she attempted to idly make small talk with me. While I appreciated the sentiment, her attempt at conversation was foiled by my utter lack of coherent thoughts at the moment. I found it arduous to converse for any length of time, the pain contorting any words I tried to convey into labored grunts and grimaces. After she listened to my racing heart, she removed her stethoscope, deftly slung it around her neck and pulled a chair up beside the head of my bed. She let me know that the doctor had ordered a few tests for me this morning, and I could expect a radiology technician to come by to pick me up in a few minutes. I gave her a look of approval and awaited the tech with a renewed hope that the upcoming tests may shed some light on the root cause of my suffering.

Reppert, Dale	DOB: 03/13/1957	Neurology Service 5 East	MR #: MA006481920
OFFICIAL HOSPITAL RECORD— Nursing Notes:	0830 hours: Large amount of liquid draining from lower incision. One suture placed		Vital Signs: 196/100 BP 110 bpm HR 24 RR 99.7 deg F Temp

Around 8:30 a.m. a man from radiology entered my room. He explained that he was going to take me down to his department to perform a CT scan of my brain and cervical spine. As he wheeled me down the hall and into the elevator, I continued to thrash around on the bed, moaning and yelling in pain. After arriving in the radiology department, I was transferred to the CT machine, which looked to me like a giant donut. The staff ordered me to lie perfectly still as they slid my head inside the center of the donut; if I wasn't able to lie perfectly still, the images would be ruined. Try as I might, I couldn't stop reflexively jerking and flailing about. I felt guilt in not being able to comply and also frustrated by their

insistence that I do so. *Couldn't they see that I was trying?* To this day, I have no idea if they were able to get the images they needed. I returned back upstairs dejected and apologetic.

I was wheeled back to my room and, upon entering, my spirits were instantly lifted as my wife was already there waiting for me. All of my anxiety and anguish was lifted if only for a brief moment. Louann was the one person in this world I could always rely on, and I was comforted by her beautiful and reassuring smile. She immediately came to the side of my bed and gingerly placed a soothing hand on my shoulder. In our marriage, I had always attempted to fill the role of the strong and steady provider. I wanted to be Louann's rock, forever her hand to hold in times of adversity. I had never planned on her seeing me like this, but I just wasn't strong enough to hide my suffering anymore. Tears welled in her eyes as she assessed my worsened condition, but she alone was able to bring me the comfort and solace that had been eluding me all night.

Dr. Andrews made his way into my room a little later Monday morning. He was sharply dressed, donning over his suit a long white coat that came down to his mid-calf. I remember reading somewhere that the length of a doctor's coat can be used to illustrate their level of training: the longer the coat, the more training they had received. That being the case, Dr. Andrews was only a few inches away from dragging his coat on the floor and was a most experienced physician. He explained to my wife and me that he needed to perform a procedure called a lumbar puncture (LP), also known to laypeople as a spinal tap. To do an LP, a 3.5 inch needle would be inserted between the bones of my spine and into the spinal canal where my spinal cord sits. The doctor would use the needle to pull out a sample of the cerebrospinal fluid, which should flow freely around my brain and spinal cord to protect them from injury. The LP is done to look for meningitis, certain types of brain bleeds, and a variety of other central nervous system disorders.

Admittedly, I wasn't thrilled with the idea of a needle the length of a ballpoint pen getting anywhere near my spinal cord, but what choice did I have? I needed answers and I had none. I probably would have let them stick a three foot needle into my back if it gave me a legitimate diagnosis and plan for recovery.

To prepare for the lumbar puncture, I was rolled onto my left side and draped with a sterile sheet. The small of my lower back was cleansed with an antiseptic sponge that smelled heavily of iodine. Cold gloved hands grasped my hips and shoulders in an attempt to stabilize my body's jerky involuntary movements. Dr. Andrews explained how imperative it was that I lay perfectly still while he was inserting the needle into my spinal canal. "Any movement at all can cause significant complications, Dale; try your best to remain still," he said.

Fear washed over my jolting body; I did not feel confident in my ability to remain still. *I couldn't do it earlier this morning in the CT scan, and now I was supposed to do better with a needle sticking into my spine?* I tried to speak up and express my concern, but my brain couldn't translate my thoughts into words fast enough; I couldn't speak. I moaned and thrashed, hoping my movement was enough to delay the needle from entering into my lower back. The gloved hands applied more pressure to my shoulders and hips, trying to force my body into compliance. The needle pierced through the top layer of my skin, and I screamed in agony, only to have the needle quickly retracted after only a few millimeters of penetration. Dr. Andrews announced we'd have to complete the procedure in the operating room under fluoroscopic guidance because there was too much movement to continue safely without further assistance.

The operating room was sterile with brilliant fluorescent lights adorning the ceiling tiles. A chill coursed through my veins as I crossed the threshold into the OR, the temperature having dropped at least 15 degrees from the hallway. I squeezed my eyes shut hoping to avoid the glare from the overhead lamp as it brightly silhouetted a small table made of chilly metal and cool black padding. Again, I was positioned on my left side with a crowd of nurses and technicians grasping at each leg, arm, and hip. I felt the weight of at least three grown adults lowering their bodies onto my legs and upper back as they struggled to keep my writhing body stationary. I was again sterilely prepped with the odoriferous iodine solution, and a second attempt was made to withdraw the fluid around my spinal cord with radiographic guidance. There was an intense pressure as the needle entered into my spinal canal with an audible pop. A purulent yellow fluid slowly dripped out of the spinal needle, thick like glue. In a normal sample of CSF, the fluid is completely colorless; in fact, it should be so clear that you could read newspaper print through the fluid. Mine looked yellowish and thick like it came out of an old bottle of wood glue.

At this point, I started to become completely oblivious to my surroundings. I was never made aware of the lumbar puncture results, or, if I had been, I didn't comprehend them. Tears swelled in my eyes as my body ached with an exhaustion that I had never before known. As I was being wheeled out of the OR, I came to the alarming realization that my mind was beginning to betray me as well. My cognizance was blunted; words became impossible to follow and thoughts difficult to form. I was no longer lucid, fading in and out of a hazy state of nothingness.

Chapter Nine
Louann: Praying for Strength

I rested my head on the doorframe outside of Dale's hospital room while Dr. Andrews attempted to perform the initial spinal tap. I only managed to stand there for a few minutes as Dale's screams were so deafening that I had to walk away; my heart couldn't bear hearing him in so much agony. I paced about thirty to forty feet down the tiled hallway only to discover that his yelling was still audible even at that distance. I found shelter in a nearby stairwell and sat helplessly on the top step with my head in my hands. I prayed for God's strength and guidance. I prayed for His presence to be with my husband and for His healing hands to guide Dr. Andrews and the hospital staff. I prayed for answers and a diagnosis. I prayed for recovery...I simply prayed.

And if we know that He hears us, whatsoever we ask, we know that we have the petitions that we desired of him. ~John 5:15 KJV

God's grace renewed me, and I steeled myself to stand up and go to comfort my loving husband. As I re-entered the room, I was informed that the initial spinal tap was unsuccessful and that the procedure needed to be performed in the operating room to help offset the risk of Dale moving during the needle insertion. Unfortunately, I was unable to accompany them down to the OR; I would have to sit upstairs and wait.

My fingers drummed rhythmically on the armrest of my chair as I anxiously wondered what could be making Dale so sick. There was probably some degree of denial involved, but I refused to let myself think about the possibility of a poor outcome. In my mind, there was no chance that anything serious was going to happen to my husband.

Dale returned to the room appearing washed out and weary. His nurse informed me that the second spinal tap was successful, and we were awaiting the results of the fluid analysis, which could take up to two hours. I gently rubbed Dale's arm, but he instantly recoiled in pain at my touch. Helplessness washed over me as I retreated to the closest chair and pulled it beside the head of his bed, "I'll be right here, honey. Hang in there, I'm praying for you."

A few minutes later, Dr. Andrews entered our room abruptly and sat down facing me, "Mrs. Reppert, I'm sure you were told that the spinal fluid results can take some time and, while that is true, the general appearance of the fluid during the lumbar puncture — the color and thickness of the fluid specifically — has me very concerned that Dale may have developed something very serious called meningitis."

"Yes, we already know that," I responded, "But I thought you said that would go away on its own."

"That's chemical meningitis, Mrs. Reppert, but I'm afraid that Dale may have contracted bacterial meningitis. They are two totally different entities. We need to get him started on antibiotics as soon as possible, and I'm recommending a transfer to the intensive care unit."

I was taken aback by the news. I didn't know much about bacterial meningitis, but I knew it was very dangerous. I vaguely recalled seeing a story on the Channel 6 News about a pretty, young college student who lost her life to bacterial meningitis a few years ago; if I remembered correctly, and I was honestly hoping I did not, she was dead within 24 hours of hospital admission. Nurses donning all-black scrubs buzzed around my husband unplugging wires and preparing him for transport to the ICU. He was out of the room and already headed downstairs before I could even wrap my head around the implications of the diagnosis. I felt like I was going to throw up.

The ICU was only two floors below me but the elevator ride took an eternity. The doors parted slowly to reveal an expansive open unit with partitions dividing up the floor into individual patient care rooms. The anterior wall of each room was made up of a sliding glass door that spanned from floor to ceiling. This design, I assumed, made it easier for the nurses to see and monitor their patients from their centralized work station. However, this also meant that while walking the corridor, I could see into every patient's room as well. It was a distressing sight; the patients in the unit looked almost sub-human with tubes protruding from every orifice, some only clinging to life by an extension cord. I felt guilty looking in their direction, as if I was never meant to see another human being in this condition. I attempted to avert my eyes and stare down at my shuffling feet, but my attention kept being drawn back upward, their torment demanding to be seen and their pain demanding to be acknowledged. Some patients lay strapped down to their beds, others kept alive by ventilator tubes taped tightly to their faces. A frail old woman lay with what looked like oversized kitchen mitts on both hands, seemingly preventing her from forcefully yanking out her tubes and IV lines; even in her fragile and barely lucid state, she still maintained the instinct to flee from a place like this. I slowed to a stop as I reached my husband's room, apprehensive to enter through the doorway. As much as I wanted to hold my husband's hand, I could only stand helplessly in the hallway looking through the glass as a bevy of nurses flurried around him to attach him to intravenous lines, medicine pumps, and monitors.

In came Dr. Rosario, a middle-aged, olive-skinned man with sympathetic brown eyes and wire rimmed glasses that continually slid downward towards the tip of his nose. I'm not sure what it was, but there was a comforting presence to the man, like an aura of light that seemed to follow him from room to room. He introduced himself as the infectious disease specialist on Dale's case and gave me a quick update on the pending spinal fluid testing, "Alright Mrs. Reppert, we have officially determined that Dale does have bacterial meningitis, but we're still waiting to see what type of bacteria caused the infection." Dr. Rosario flipped open the deep burgundy plastic chart that hung at the foot of Dale's bed and leafed through the previous day's notes, mumbling softly to himself while tapping his foot, "Ok, yes, this is fine…vitals, yup, ok, on the right meds, perfect…still awaiting the culture and gram stain, repeat labs, alright… " he trailed off as he closed

Dale's medical chart, "Ok, now Mrs. Reppert, I know this is a lot to take in. Do you have any questions for me?"

Oh, I had a zillion questions. This all progressed so quickly that I barely even had time to think. Just yesterday morning my husband was at home with me, and now today he's practically unresponsive in an ICU. *Yeah, I had questions.* Yet before I was able to speak, I caught the sight of Dale's head slowly turning towards me, like he was searching for me. It actually almost looked like he wanted to tell me something. I immediately stood up and rushed to the side of his bed, "Dale, what is it honey? Is everything okay?"

His eyes locked directly on mine, and he remarkably began to speak, only mumbles at first, but then I thought I could begin to make out actual words, "Lou, call my assistant, I need to check up on the PPL stock."

Are you freaking kidding me? He hasn't spoken a coherent sentence all day and now he's trying to do work? "That's not important right now, Dale. We need to focus on getting you better, okay? Your clients will understand."

Dale stared blankly past me, not even acknowledging my response. His muttering began again, this time only lasting for a few brief seconds and ending with a comment that a Personal Pan Pizza from Pizza Hut sounded reaaally good to him right now.

I let out a small laugh, the first in a few days, as a large smile spread across my face; maybe Dale was actually improving. This morning he struggled to even find a singular word, and now he just spoke a few articulate sentences. Sure, his ramblings were a bit odd, but Dale loved his job and he loved Pizza Hut. Who was I to judge the things he thought about while he was sick?

Upon seeing my unbridled excitement, Dr. Rosario gently touched my arm and led me into the hallway. He glanced back at Dale, trying to determine if he was far enough away not to be heard, "Louann, I need you to recognize how critical Dale's condition is right now. These next 24 to 48 hours are going to determine whether your husband lives or dies. Do you have any other family members here with you?"

Wait, hang on a second. What? I was unable to register what Dr. Rosario had just told me. Despite the diagnosis, I had still wholly assumed that Dale would be fine and home with the family within a few days, a week at most. Dale had faced other serious health scares throughout his life and had always been fortunate enough to bounce back quickly without any lasting issues. I hadn't yet considered that this time might be different.

Once Dale was fully settled in his ICU room, I quickly ran back to the house so I could be home when the kids got off the school bus. Our oldest, Taryn, was away at college taking finals, but I still had to make arrangements for Tristin and Tyler for the evening. Luckily, longtime family friends, Kim and Paul, offered to have both children over for a nice home-cooked dinner and a movie night so that I could get back to the hospital to be with Dale.

After seeing that the kids were taken care of, I was forced to deal with the unpleasant task of calling Dale's family to update them on his condition. I hated being the bearer of bad news and, to make things worse, I didn't really understand what was going on or how serious his condition had become. I tried to use the doctor's exact words as much as possible. My first call was to Dale's father, Bill. Bill had been living in Florida by himself for the past two years since Dale's mom passed away unexpectedly. We didn't get to see Bill often; in fact, we hadn't seen him since the day of Mary's funeral. Dale and his brothers never had a particularly close relationship with their father. There was silence on the other end of the line as I explained Dale's worsening condition, finally finishing with a short upbeat speech I'd prepared about his son being a trooper and how I had the utmost faith in God's ability to get him through this tough time. I nervously awaited his response, "Bill... are you still there?"

"I'm coming up there. I'll let you know the details later, but I'm coming up there as soon as I can get a flight. Thanks for calling, Louann. I'll be seeing you soon, bye."

After hanging up with Bill, I had similar short conversations with Dale's brothers, Steve and Todd, both of whom lived down south in Oklahoma and Texas respectively. I then decided to make the fifteen minute drive over to Pizza Hut. While I realized that Dale's request earlier in the hospital room was probably just the medicine talking or some weird manifestation of delirium, I still wanted to get him that personal pan pizza he craved. As helpless as I felt, this was one tangible thing I could do for my husband that might help him feel better or at least bring a smile to his face. Just the idea of eating pizza with my husband offered me a small glimmer of hope for an eventual return to our normal life. I gleefully envisioned my husband seated beside me in his favorite beat-up old t-shirt and running shorts, pouring entirely too much salt onto his pizza and laughing loudly at some Seinfeld re-run he'd already seen a million times. A mundane moment that I'd witnessed a hundred times before in our relationship now seemed like the absolute pinnacle of bliss. There's a lot of beauty to be found in life's ordinary moments if you're willing to open your eyes and look for them. I couldn't help but feel a bit ashamed that it took something so traumatic to make me aware of this.

I left Pizza Hut and headed straight back to the ICU, personal pan pizza in tow. As I entered Dale's room, I instantly felt my heart race as a swell of warm blood rushed to my cheeks in embarrassment. *Oh my God, I must be in the wrong room.* I walked in to see a half-naked man fully exposing his rear-end and mooning the entire hallway through the open windows. I muttered a quick apology and hurriedly attempted to reverse out of the room, feeling awkwardly as if I had just walked in on someone using the restroom. There was no way that could have been my modest husband. *Why would the hospital change his room without telling me?* I rerouted to the nurse's station to inquire about my husband's new room. To my disbelief, they informed me that the half-naked man showing his butt off to everyone was Dale.

A young blonde technician with kind eyes and blue scrubs was seated to the left of Dale's bed. "What's going on?" I asked her, "How long has he been like this?"

"Shortly after you left he became delirious and kept trying to pull out his IVs and his catheter. Someone has to sit with him at all times to make sure he doesn't hurt himself or interfere with treatment."

"And that's you?"

"Yes, Mrs. Reppert."

"Well, is it okay if I tie his gown on him a little better?" I said as I moved slowly towards Dale's bed. "He would have a fit if he knew he was flashing himself to the entire hospital."

"Absolutely, Mrs. Reppert."

"Thanks."

Dale spoke out randomly as if he was having conversations with multiple different people, despite the fact that only the tech and I were in the room.

"Hey Tristin, tie your shoes…I don't want to see you fall down on the court," he coached out loud to no one. The entire scene was so incredibly odd and upsetting. *What was going on inside his head?* The outbursts kept getting stranger and stranger until they finally culminated with Dale yelling out that Michael Jackson was hiding in his closet. His room didn't even have a closet. At this nonsense, I went over to talk with him but sadly saw no glimmer of recognition in his eyes. My husband had no idea who I was. Reflexively, I tried to comfort him by resting my hand on his upper arm, but he violently pushed me away and grabbed at his IV line instead. The tech beside him bolted up out of her chair to swiftly restrain his hands. She spoke to him as if he was a child, and he responded as such with a string of incoherent babbles and groans.

At that moment, just as Dale's delirium had become truly terrifying, our friend Mike, who worked at the hospital, decided to pop in to see how we were doing. I immediately burst into tears, so relieved to see a familiar face as my entire world was crashing down around me. I threw my arms around him and wrapped him in a giant bear hug, "I am so glad you're here."

Mike is a wonderful obstetrician and a truly calming presence. Having delivered two of our children and talked me down off the edge more than a few times throughout the entire birthing process, I figured if anyone could get Dale to relax, it would be Dr. Mike. However, despite Mike's and my best efforts, Dale remained acutely agitated and continued to carry out incoherent conversations with the air around him.

Too quickly, the announcement came that visiting hours were ending, and I left after telling Dale how much I loved him, not knowing if he actually understood me or even recognized who I was.

I cried the entire way home.

Chapter Ten
Letting Go

There came a moment on Monday afternoon, after Louann had gone home to make arrangements for the kids, that I laid in my bed and consciously felt my life slipping away from me. I had lost all ability to fight. I still had no knowledge of what was wrong with me. I wasn't aware that I had bacterial meningitis, and I knew nothing of the septic shock and early multi-system organ dysfunction that followed. I just knew of the pain. My mind became a slave to the physical torment, and I felt as if I couldn't bear another minute of the suffering. Throughout my life, I had prided myself on my physical conditioning, consistently training myself for an unknown battle and knowing I would always be ready for whatever life threw at me. *I was wrong.* This was stronger than I was; I was losing the battle for my own life. Through a fog of despair, I experienced a fleeting moment of lucidity, like a revelation from God himself. For the first time, I clearly recognized that certain activities, which had consumed so much of my life and almost wholly defined my identity, were utterly insignificant and superficial. While lying on my literal "death bed," my thoughts were not of business, work, or clients, but of my wife and three children, wonderful moments we had spent together, and an intense desire to create many more such memories.

As I lay there losing my war to pain and confusion, a cloak of fear enveloped me. I was scared to lose Louann and my three wonderful children. I needed the chance to say goodbye, to wrap them all up in my arms and let them how much I loved them, and to apologize for not being there as much as I should have been. The mental and physical torture overpowered me, and I begged for salvation from the unendurable pain. I prayed for the strength and courage to follow whatever desires the Lord had planned for me. And then came the feeling that I was finally ready. In that singular moment, my fear suddenly transformed into an overwhelming sense of peace and tranquility. A powerful force cradled every inch of my body as I made the conscious decision to let go of Louann and my family and turn myself over to the calming embrace of God. My prayers had been answered.

For I reckon that the sufferings of this present time are not worthy to be compared with the glory which shall be revealed to us. ~ Romans 8:18 KJV

Chapter Eleven
Louann: Halos and Head Wounds

My husband still didn't recognize me when I returned to the ICU on Tuesday morning. Looking into his eyes again only to see pure nothingness felt like a punch to the gut. His eyes were fully open but unseeing, hollowed out like there was no one home inside. *Where are you Dale?* I couldn't be sure where my sweet husband was at that point, but he certainly wasn't lying in that hospital bed in front of me.

Shortly after my arrival, a team from the hospital asked me to join them for a meeting about Dale's condition. I was thankful to have my friend Kim along with me for some much needed moral support. The team of doctors was trying to figure out why they couldn't control Dale's agitation levels or induce sleep with the sedating medications they had been using on him. "Mrs. Reppert, are you aware of your husband having any history of illicit drug use?"

Kim nearly laughed out loud, "Dale using hard drugs? Oh my gosh, could you imagine?"

My husband had never so much as picked up a cigarette and only drank alcohol, usually a strawberry daiquiri topped with a big dollop of whipped cream, maybe once every ten years.

When he was in college, people used to give him a hard time about not wanting to drink, but he never wavered.

I'd always admired that about him — even from a young age, he was strong in his convictions. Most kids would have crumbled under the weight of adolescent peer-pressure, but Dale was so comfortable in his own skin that he never once caved. He didn't want to drink, so he didn't drink; it was as simple as that.

I tried to explain Dale's longstanding history of sobriety to the hospital staff, but they still insisted on a full screening panel, testing for a multitude of drugs that were unfamiliar to both Kim and me. Although I didn't agree with the testing, I understood the doctor's plight and assumed that many people lied when asked this question. As I knew they would be, all the results came back negative.

I spent the rest of the morning sitting quietly with Dale, staring blankly at a shell of what used to be my steadfast husband. He was lost in pain, miserably trapped in his own tortured world, unable to be set free. I watched his pale form thrash around the bed for hours until Dr. Mike and his wife Carolyn came in to visit. Devoted Catholics, they came bearing holy water, anointing Dale's forehead with a few drops and the sign of the cross. Carolyn read Saint Joseph's Prayer from a pocket-sized laminated card she had brought to give to Dale:

PRAYER TO SAINT JOSEPH

Joseph, like the people of your time, and like us today, you were familiar with doubt, worry, anguish and suffering. Your desire was to be attentive to the manifestations of God's will. Help us to identify how we can best overcome our difficulties...

Remember, O most chaste spouse of the Virgin Mary, that never has it been known that anyone who asked for your help and sought your intercession was left unaided...

✝ ✝ ✝

"...Remember, O most chaste spouse of the Virgin Mary, that never has it been known that anyone who asked for your help and sought your intercession was left unaided..."

Carolyn, Mike, and I stood together around Dale's bed, lowered our heads, and prayed solemnly that the Lord lift Dale up, comfort him in times of pain, renew his strength, and bring peace to his body and his soul. I didn't realize it at the time, but my two close friends, both of whom were medical professionals, didn't expect my husband to make it through the night.

After Mike and Carolyn left, I sat vigil for hours next to Dale's bed, helpless, overwhelmed and almost delirious myself from sleep deprivation. Mike came back again later towards the end of his shift to see if anything had changed. "Still unresponsive," I shrugged weakly.

Mike and I conversed for a few minutes until we heard a voice cut through the chatter; it was Dale. He looked directly at Mike and me and for the first time since yesterday, signs of life flickered inside his icy blue eyes. He pointed to the space above both our heads and breathed the words, "Bright lights," and then began chanting, "Halos, halos, halos…" as he circled his finger knowingly in our direction. I wasn't sure if I should be happy or crushed. While it was wonderful to hear my husband's voice again, I was frightened by the subject matter. To me, bright lights and halos meant I was only one step away from losing my husband's earthly presence.

I ran home to check on the kids and hurriedly fixed myself a grilled cheese sandwich, the first solid meal I'd had in days. When I returned to the hospital that evening around 7:00 pm, Dale's words of halos and lights were replaced solely with moans of anguish and expressions of terror. I walked in to find Dale's new nursing technician, a petite young girl with shiny brown hair, positioned at the head of his bed with her back to me. Upon hearing me enter the room, she startled and glanced quickly in my direction, her eyes gleaming with fresh tears. "Oh honey, what's the matter? Are you okay?" I asked as I dropped my belongings and went to throw my arm around the young girl's shoulder. I made it two steps from the bed before I realized what had been distressing the inexperienced tech. I recoiled in horror as I witnessed rhythmic spurts of bright red blood shooting out from Dale's head incision. The tech's white gloves were drenched in blood, and a small mountain of deep crimson gauze pads lay balled up on the bedside table beside her. All at once, I became acutely aware of my heart thumping in my chest, I blinked tightly as the lateral fields of my vision blurred, and my head became light and airy. My skin flushed with a prickly heat, and I began to sweat profusely as I stumbled backwards and crashed into a plastic visitor's chair. I quickly sat and dropped my head between my knees hoping to ward off the eventual loss of consciousness that was sure to follow. Panicked, I heard the tech sprint from the room leaving both Dale and I alone and in distress.

Three nurses barreled into the room, jolting me back to awareness and fighting to control the bleeding from my husband's incision with direct pressure and elevation. The spurting blood immediately soaked though the gauze pads, transforming each one from fresh white to deep red within an instant. A full fifteen minutes passed before the nurses were able to control the acute bleeding. Miraculously, Dale was still alive.

Still in shock, I remained by Dale's bedside and ineffectually tried to comfort him until visiting hours ended for the night. I wasn't sure what I was supposed to do. I had no idea how to be the strong one anymore, having ceded that role to my husband long ago. In times of trouble, the kids and I all looked to him for guidance and support. *Was I supposed to be the rock for myself and our family? Who could I turn to?* I needed God's strength to support me, to hold me up and help me to be strong for my children and Dale. I broke down in the hospital parking garage before the half-hour drive home, crying for the man that I loved, the illness that was taking him away from me, and the helplessness I felt that I couldn't save him. After wiping the final tear, I took a deep breath and steeled myself to return home, knowing full well that I now needed to be the rock for my family.

Chapter Twelve
Heaven

We assume and, quite frankly, take for granted the fact that we will awaken each morning to experience the gift of another day. By mid-afternoon on Monday, I began questioning whether or not I'd actually live long enough to see the sun rise the next morning. Imagine tonight, before you close your eyes and drift off to sleep, that you will not awaken tomorrow morning. What would it change about the way you're living your life? What things would you want to tell those closest to you? For me, each ticking second took on new meaning and value.

It's difficult to explain what it feels like to have your life slip through your fingers. It's surreal; you have an awareness that you are actively dying, yet there is absolutely nothing you can do to prevent it. You are a spectator watching your own life play out with no ability to influence the outcome. I saw my own mind laid out like a giant hourglass and was forced to watch as each little trace of my cognition filtered down through to the bottom of the glass, never to be utilized again. Images flashed one by one in my mind. Family memories passed by so quickly that I barely had time to register them. A fleeting image of Louann smiling at me on our first date, Taryn's amazement at her first step, Tristin's smile and infectious laugh, the joy in seeing my son's birth. I saw nothing of material possessions or work successes. I only saw the people that I loved the most in this world, and I ached to create more memories with them.

As the last few recognizable thoughts and memories passed through my mind, I finally lost the will to survive. As I relinquished all thoughts of continuing, a wave of peace and tranquility overcame my body. I felt as if God himself had placed me in his loving care. At the very moment I lost control of my ability to communicate with this world, I became connected to something far greater than myself. The agonizing pain I experienced over the past three days was fully erased, and I was cradled in a loving and warm embrace.

I sought the LORD, and he heard me, and delivered me from my fears.
~PSALM 34:4 KJV

While I may have appeared agitated and confused to those who visited me in the hospital from May 5th to May 7th, I was actually residing in a place of perfect peace. I have no memory of any sickness or physical pain. I do not recall the traumatic opening of my incision or the immediacy in which I was rushed to emergency life-saving surgery. I only remember the light.

The journey that I am about to speak of was, without question, the most profound experience of my entire life. The events that took place over the forty-five hours from Monday evening to Wednesday afternoon would detour my life forever. While I always believed in God, I had never experienced anything strong enough to turn my blind faith into knowing certainty, until this happened.

****

It all begins with a hazy white light surrounding the outlines of people in my hospital room. There is an aura-like quality to the light, as if it is actually emanating from the silhouettes themselves. Faces have become impossible to recognize through the thick white haze, but the forms beneath them are distinctly human. The auras float slowly around the room following no particular pattern, and as new forms enter or exit at will, they are seemingly free to roam as they wish. All at once, a brilliant, yet gently soft, white beam of light begins to sprout out from the horizon, reaching upward until it forms into a roof-like dome. The hazy light is mesmerizing, and I find myself enraptured, unable to stop staring, as the dense fog slowly encapsulates my entire body until it is all I can see.

As if all at once, the light swallows me up completely, and immediately there is no more pain. The foggy, yet stunning cloud of light goes on indefinitely, stretching endlessly around me in every direction. This light no longer causes me any pain and doesn't even cause me to squint. It feels like it is made of the purest and deepest love I could ever imagine, carrying with it a joy that brightens every inch of my world and strengthens my spirit. In front of my eyes, I begin to make out the faces of loved ones who I have previously lost. Their faces smile at me, softly, gently, and ever so peacefully. Everyone looks amazing, all appearing much younger than I recall them being at the time of their deaths. Surprisingly, not one of them appears to be older than fifty, and they all look healthy, even those who I know had spent their later years ravaged by crippling illness and disease. They are now in the prime of their lives, truly vibrant and alive, wearing reassuring smiles and expressions that let me know everything is going to be okay.

I see the faces of my dear mother, grandfather, uncle, and grandmother, among a few other family members I don't fully recognize. While all of these individuals had different temperaments in life, they all offer the same consoling, comforting smiles here in this place.

My mother's face is the closest to me, slightly off to my left. It is wonderful to see her smile again, so at ease and comfortable. I honestly can't remember the last time I saw her smile like that, it must be at least twenty or more years ago. During the last few decades of her life, my mother suffered from debilitating arthritis that forced her to live in constant pain. Smiles were infrequent; her face more often found contorted into a pained scowl. She died suddenly at the age of 71 after succumbing to an accidental overdose of chlorine gas while trying to clean her pool. It wasn't an easy death, yet here she appears to be finally free from all of the pain, fully at peace and happy. Her face no longer holds the wrinkles of old age or the deeply cut lines of daily grimacing; she looks as she did on my wedding day in 1980. She looks beautiful.

To my right is my Uncle Ray. His round, moon-like, face smiles at me in the most reassuring and encouraging way. He looks to be in his mid-forties, roughly thirty years younger than the age he died. Uncle Ray was a laid-back fella, always laughing and joking around with everyone. In this place, he appears to be downright giddy, like he is waiting for the opportunity to horse around with me and act like a kid again.

My paternal grandmother, Katie, is also on my right. From what I knew of her, she was tough as nails, a single mother to my father and his two siblings. Katie's husband, my grandfather, passed away suddenly when my dad was eleven.

To my surprise I see my grandfather Roy smiling at me. My mother's father wasn't necessarily a terrible guy, but he was known to have made some questionable decisions. In his youth, he abandoned his duties as a father and walked out on his wife and children, forcing my mother and aunt to live out their childhoods in an orphanage. Later in life, he returned to make amends with my mother and she somehow found it in her heart to forgive him. Although he was always pleasant to me, I found it difficult to respect him. *How do you just walk out on your family like that?* While my grandpa was a hard-worker and even owned his own business, he never struck me as the most moral of men; he appeared to live a selfish life filled with womanizing and drinking to excess. I don't know what the exact qualifications are to make it to this place, but I know that God doesn't make any mistakes. Grandpa Roy is here for a reason, and I am truly happy for the guy, a bit surprised, yes, but happy.

As I continue to scan the various faces, there are many I cannot decipher because they are too far in the distance. While some of these people are close family members, others are complete strangers to me. Yet regardless of our relationship to one another, each person's image is immensely calming to me. Never have I felt such tranquility or perfect peace. The brilliant light and comforting visages completely rid me of all pain, fear, and anxiety. The stress I had previously felt regarding the potential loss of my wife and children has vanished only to be replaced by an all-encompassing serenity more wonderful than anything I ever could have imagined. Although none of the figures physically speak to me, their mere presence communicates an amazing sense of safety and security that assures me that everything is even better than okay. I know with great certainty that I am in Heaven, or at the very least, Heaven's waiting room.

Looking back, the mere thought of this experience is enough to bring a smile to my face and a tear to my eye. I believe it was God's intervention, a way to temporarily alleviate my suffering in order to save my life. While my body was being relentlessly beaten and bloodied back on earth, He chose to lift me up and place my spirit into Heaven's loving embrace for nearly two full days. I was given a glimpse of something more beautiful than anything I could have ever dreamed. Not many people get to experience something like this. I know that I was in Heaven and, because of this, my life is forever changed. There's a certain peace to me now that I never possessed before; I no longer fear death or what's to come of me after leaving this world.

I know that I will return to Heaven one day when God decides He's ready for me.

Chapter Thirteen
Louann: Emergency Surgery

I awoke abruptly to the sound of the telephone ringing at 5 o'clock early Wednesday morning. I immediately bolted upright in my bed with a realization that made my heart sink: This call most likely concerned Dale. I jumped out of bed and ran to the phone. Sure enough, it was Dr. Andrews on the other end of the line, "What happened?" I got out breathlessly, "Is everything okay with Dale?"

"He needs emergency surgery, Louann. The infection spread to his blood stream, and he's going into septic shock. His blood pressure is all over the place and isn't responding to the usual therapies; we need to act now before his organs start to fail."

"Ok...um...ok," I stammered. "When is the surgery? Can I see him first?"

"Unfortunately, he's already back there being prepped. His incision opened up again this morning, and we had a tough time controlling the bleeding, so we had to intervene a little bit faster than we would have liked to."

At that, Dr. Andrews excused himself and handed me off to one of his physician assistants (PA) so I could get some more information. According to the PA, the best chance they had to save Dale's life was to bring him back to the operating room and essentially repeat the entire duraplasty procedure, removing the infected patch from the lining of his brain and replacing it with a brand new patch. He most likely wouldn't survive the way things were progressing; we had no choice but to repeat the procedure.

On the way to the hospital, I phoned my minister and asked if he would pray for my husband. He offered to come sit with me while Dale was in surgery, and I graciously accepted hoping his calming presence and prayer would help me get through the arduous wait. Once at the hospital I found myself needing to be alone for a moment to gather my thoughts. Everything had been so frantic lately that I had been operating on a form of autopilot, a fight or flight response, if you will. Every action and decision I made was devoid of emotion; my only focus being on the survival of my family and my husband. I leaned back in my padded chair, took a deep breath, and closed my eyes. The situation was entirely in God's hands.

I thought back to the last time I was in a similar situation, helplessly waiting in a room like this and praying for my husband. It was fourteen years ago. Dale was thirty-six and about to undergo a thoracotomy to remove a baseball-sized mass from his right lung. It was assumed that the mass was cancerous, so we were prepared to have the entire lung removed if it came down to that. I wanted to know exactly what we were getting into so I did a little bit of research on the procedure at the public library. *Big mistake.* The thoracotomy sounded brutal, barbaric even, involving a giant ten-inch incision and then the use of a stainless steel rib-spreader to gain access to the lung. *I couldn't even imagine how much that would hurt.* The surgery took place on our son Tyler's first birthday and I was a nervous wreck, cursing myself for learning the specifics of the procedure. About an hour into the surgery, a woman in scrubs ambled through the doorway and addressed the waiting room, "Is there a Louann Reppert in here?"

I immediately feared the worst, my stomach doubling itself into knots. *They shouldn't be calling me this early; something terrible must have happened. I'll bet the rib spreader punctured his lung. Oh God.*

She could sense my fear, and quickly informed me that everything was okay; she just had a delivery for me. I was floored when she handed over a box filled with a dozen long-stemmed roses and a card that simply read, "I love you - Dale." I immediately began to tear up, absolutely in awe of the man I married, a man who, while on his way into major surgery, was thinking of ways to make his wife feel better in the waiting room.

Four hours later, the surgeon emerged from the operating room with the most wonderful news. To his great surprise, the tumor was not cancerous after all, but rather an inflammatory tumor from a rare disease called Sarcoidosis. The surgeon was able to fully resect the tumor, and Dale got to keep his right lung. Everything was a success. While the surgery was a major one, requiring a full week of hospitalization and a three-month recovery period, my husband would survive. He did not have invasive lung cancer.

Following this miraculous turn of events, Dale vowed to alter his working hours to spend more time with his family. There would be no more weekends spent working on client accounts or trying to gain new business on the golf course. Saturdays would be strictly for family time, and Sundays we would hire a babysitter and devote the day to dating each other again like we did before we had children.

I knew there would be no roses in the waiting room for me today as I bowed my head to pray. I prayed for Dale's recovery, for our struggling family, and for more Saturdays and Sundays.

The entire emergency surgery took approximately four hours, but it felt more like forty. I leapt out of my chair when I saw Dr. Andrews enter the waiting room, assessing his facial expression to make a split second determination of how the surgery had gone. *Well he doesn't look upset, but then again, he doesn't look particularly happy either.* I held my breath.

"The procedure went well but Dale's still not out of the woods yet. We took out the synthetic Gor-Tex patch from the lining of his brain and replaced it with a bovine patch."

"A bovine patch?" I questioned. "Like, you mean bovine as in cow?"

"Yes, the patches are made from the lining of a cow's heart actually."

"Strange."

"They work quite well actually, very inexpensive yet strong with minimal elasticity."

I couldn't believe Dale now had part of a cow heart covering his brain. *He was totally going to get a kick out of that; I couldn't wait to tell him about it when he woke up.*

During the procedure, Dr. Andrews soaked Dale's brain in an antibiotic solution before closing the incision, hoping to kill any bacteria still present in the meningeal layer. He mentioned that while the IV antibiotics were successfully attacking the bacteria in his bloodstream, they did little to kill the bacteria on the patch itself, thus allowing the infection to continue to proliferate. Removing the patch was essentially cutting off the infection at its source.

I was the only one allowed back to see Dale in the recovery room; I couldn't even bring my minister with me. I didn't even recognize the man that lay before me; he looked nothing like my husband. Dale was tied down to the bed like an animal, half of his face drooped downward as if being pulled by a heavy weight, a small puddle of drool collecting on the pillowcase under his right cheek. He was still under the fog of anesthesia and looked absolutely dreadful, perhaps the worst I'd ever seen him. *I didn't even think it was possible to look worse than he did last night, but he does.*

Dale awoke in a fog two days later in the ICU, the right side of his face still drooping terribly. I felt certain he had suffered a stroke during the procedure; there was no other explanation as to why his face was still so asymmetrical. When he opened his mouth to try to speak, only the left side of his lips moved while the right side appeared pinned down in place. His words were unintelligible, jumbled, and slurred.

For the next few days, Dale didn't talk much. He stared off into space and seemed incapable of making eye contact. I continued to speak to him as if he was still with me, discussing Tyler and Tristin's schedules, school projects, tennis matches, and how Taryn was doing on finals. Maybe he could understand me; I didn't know. At one point, he looked directly at me; I smiled broadly in return, only to then witness his eyes roll back into their sockets. He became fully unresponsive to outside stimuli as I frantically yelled and cried, "Help! Somebody please help me!"

This episode was a seizure and Dale had been having them intermittently ever since he came out of the emergency surgery. He had already been started on two different anti-seizure medications in order to combat them, but the medicine wasn't helping. Each seizure lasted only a few minutes, which felt like an eternity. I felt so helpless watching Dale and could only sit there wringing my hands and praying for each seizure to pass.

The next few days of Dale's recovery were slow going. He looked exhausted and got very little sleep while in the ICU. His room was directly beside the helicopter landing-pad, and the whirring of helicopter blades and the commotion from incoming traumas would consistently awaken him throughout the night. After a long week in the ICU, filled with plenty of touch-and-go moments, Dale's doctors decided it was finally safe to move him to the neurological unit on the fourth floor.

Before Dale left the ICU, one of the nurses he'd been particularly fond of came in to see him off. The nurse was a seasoned veteran of the intensive care unit, with over seventeen years of critical care experience. He mentioned to me that Dale's case had been one of the most miraculous recoveries he had ever witnessed throughout his career. "I thought for sure your husband was a goner, Mrs. Reppert," he remarked to me as he went to go shake Dale's hand, "You're one stubborn old Dutchman, Mr. Reppert, you know that? Take care of yourself."

****

Dale: Sent Back

My eyes open to the harsh glare of overhead lights, and I immediately shut them again tightly. My head throbs incessantly as I try to blink away the confusion and grogginess; I feel very disoriented. *Where the heck am I?* Blurry faces and human forms materialize from the light, and I gradually begin to become aware of my surroundings again. *This is a hospital room. What's going on? This looks like a recovery room. Why am I in a recovery room again?*

I attempt to move my arms, but they are tightly fastened to bed rails by restraints. Something plastic in my mouth prevents me from speaking or screaming. An intense feeling of confusion and panic gives way to an utterly devastating sense of disappointment and loss. While only a few moments ago, I bathed in the warm spiritual embrace of loved ones and light, I now am apparently back in the cold sterile hospital, in pain, and all alone.

Harried thoughts swirl in my mind. A memory of excruciating pain and a realization of imminent death both surface and mix with the concrete sensation of having been to a heavenly place. *Did I die? Am I dying still?*

I move fluidly between conscious thoughts and unconsciousness, with jarring moments of fear and confusion. I am lost, disconnected from ordinary life and all human communication.

Chapter Fourteen
Louann: Hospital Recovery

Once Dale was relocated to the fourth floor, he was able to get some much-needed rest. Moving from the ICU to a more "normal" room appeared to lift his spirits considerably. While he was still quite ill and receiving heavy doses of pain medication and antibiotics around the clock, the minute-to-minute worrying about his survival seemed to have passed. We could now turn some of our attention towards actively recovering instead of just escaping death.

Our middle daughter Tristin had left for Florida the Monday before Dale's second surgery. She had been invited to attend the local school prom with a friend. I hadn't told her of the severity of her father's illness, trying to shelter her from worry. She came home from Florida two days after the second surgery and immediately went to visit her father in the hospital. She was shocked to see how ill and frail he looked and was furious with me for not telling her how critical the situation had become in her brief absence. Looking back on it now, I regret not being fully honest with my children about their father's grim state. In my mind, I was trying to protect them from the harsh reality of the situation and all the worrying and stress that comes with having a critically ill parent. I worried that my children couldn't handle it. I know now that I was wrong; I shouldn't have kept them in the dark. They never would have forgiven me had something happened to Dale and they didn't get the chance to say goodbye to their father. I don't think I could have forgiven myself either.

Each child dealt with Dale's illness in their own different way. Taryn was away at college and somewhat removed from the situation, but she was always a sympathetic ear and listened to me attentively when things got stressful at home. Tyler probably had the hardest time coping with his father's illness; he struggled seeing his strong father confined to a hospital bed, and he completely shut down emotionally every time he entered the hospital. Tristin was the caregiver. She took it upon herself to set aside her high school tennis career and other extracurricular activities for the entirety of Dale's hospitalization so she could come by every day after school to help her father recover. She fed him, changed his sheets, and encouraged him daily in his recovery.

Dale had become so weak that the staff had to teach him how to walk again. The rehab nurses tasked Tris and I with making sure he got out of the room to do his daily laps around the nurses station. Tris would grab his left arm, I'd grab his right, and we'd push around his IV pole as he slowly shuffled his feet between us. It was tough to watch him start over again like this. Before meningitis, Dale was an avid runner and logged anywhere from 25 to 30 miles a week; now, we were cheering wildly when he completed three good steps in a row.

Dale's father flew in from Florida to stay with us during his son's recovery, which meant the world to Dale. I never saw Dale and his father truly express how much they loved or respected one another, but I assumed that was a normal father-son relationship. Bill's being there spoke volumes about the love he had for his son, even if he didn't always express it verbally. He would help Dale shower and shave, brush his teeth, and feed him gently like a child. Throughout adulthood, I'd watched Dale and his father slowly grow apart, Dale trying to distance himself from the man who raised him, promising he'd never be as unemotional towards his children as his father was to him and his brothers. As I watched Bill lather and shave his forty-six year-old son, I could see their emotional bond strengthening each day.

Dale's frequent seizures continued daily despite the cocktail of anti-seizure medications he'd been taking. After each seizure, he appeared exhausted, as if the seizure had sapped every ounce of energy from him. The only thing that Dale enjoyed during this period of his recovery was watching mindless television. Anything that was too intellectually stimulating was overwhelming to him; he couldn't complete his crossword puzzles, play Sudoku, or finish word games like he did in the past. He was like a child, home sick from school, watching daytime television and loving every second of it. His favorite show was essentially every child's favorite show to watch on a sick day: "The Price is Right" with Bob Barker. My husband was captivated by that game-show. He yelled out prices at the screen as if he was actually a contestant on the show and had prizes on the line. From his hospital bed he would enthusiastically shout out, "One Dollar, Bob," if he believed everyone on the panel had overbid. I watched more episodes of "The Price is Right" in those two weeks than I had in my entire life. Honestly, I'd be fine if I never watched another episode again; it takes me right back to Dale's time in the hospital and stirs up too many bad memories.

Chapter Fifteen
Heading Home

I remember very little of my stay in the ICU, although I do distinctly recall being annoyed by the helicopter noise. Without fail, any time I would finally manage to fall asleep, the whirr of helicopter blades from the emergency helipad would suddenly jar me awake. Funny how the one thing I remember from my life-saving surgery and ICU stay is being annoyed.

I learned from Louann that I first became conscious and spoke on Friday, two days after my second surgery. My first words were about my mother and bright lights, but no one understood what I was saying. Apparently, I really wanted to tell everyone what I'd seen in Heaven but wasn't quite capable of articulating it yet. At this point, I was aware of my wife's presence beside me. What a comfort it was to hold her hand and see her smile again! The loneliness and feelings of isolation I had felt upon awakening in the recovery room had instantly diminished.

Of the few memories I retained from my two weeks in the hospital, the faithful presence of my wife, father, and children at my bedside will always remain with me. They consistently encouraged me, supported me mentally and emotionally, and helped assist with my physical needs. My father, who was typically distant and unemotional, helped me tremendously. His willingness to be there for me and support me through the toughest struggle of my life meant a great deal to me. During those days, a new and stronger relationship with my father was forged.

While the support of my family gave me strength, I wasn't blind to their worries. I could not blame them; their concern was certainly warranted. I was beginning to experience difficulties in everyday conversation. I struggled to remember names and even form coherent thoughts at times. I would forget what certain household objects were called, and I'd frequently mix up words when trying to speak. I tried not to let it worry me, hoping it was just part of the recovery process, but I could tell by the looks on their faces that my family was deeply bothered by it.

I began to recognize the severity of my illness on the first day of hospital physical therapy. The doctors had suggested that I should start trying to get out of bed in order to get my body moving and keep my strength up. After lunch, I was taken by wheelchair to a small room situated at the end of my hallway. An energetic and hopeful physical therapist met me inside. She introduced herself as Annie and pointed over to my first exercise of the day: a small step, approximately four to five inches off the ground, with handlebars adorning its sides. I was to simply step up on to the platform and then step down. *Yup, that was it. That was the "exercise."* I softly chuckled to myself. *All right Annie, if you say so.* As she helped me out of my wheelchair, I quickly realized that my brain wasn't able to deliver messages to the rest of my body like it used to do without much thought. Previously, my body just did what I wanted it to do automatically, but now, the amount of mental focus it took to simply move each limb was astounding. Perhaps I underestimated just how difficult this recovery was going to be.

As anyone in the hospital could tell you, the big highlight of my day was getting to watch "The Price is Right" at 11:00 a.m. The absolute best days for me were ones when a contestant was lucky enough to get to play Plinko. I have no idea what it was about that game, but I couldn't stop staring at the descending disks and trying to guess which prize value they'd end up landing in. I'd even make little side bets with Louann. "Lou, Lou," I'd gleefully shout, "I'll bet this lady gets it in the $1000!" I can only assume my wife was annoyed by my behavior, but she didn't say so at the time. Even if she had, I wasn't really in any condition to notice. My mannerisms and behavior had become increasingly more child-like since the surgery. In our strolls through the halls, I took pleasure in shooting the "thumbs-up" sign to every patient and visitor I walked past, complete with a goofy lopsided grin.

Physically, strange things were occurring as well. I experienced vision problems where the left half of my visual field had just disappeared and was replaced with a huge black box. The right side of my face consistently felt droopy, weak, and numb like I had just left the dentist. I also drooled quite frequently out of the right side of my mouth. My head still ached constantly, but the pain was very manageable compared to what I was used to. It went from my pre-surgery, "TEN," to a minuscule little three. Alleluia! I could deal with a three. Fortunately for me, I was unaware of the seizures which overtook my body frequently throughout each day. To me, they were just blank lapses in time. The only way I could even tell that I had had a seizure was the overwhelming fatigue that followed each episode, but even that was manageable; I just slept it off.

Though still experiencing significant disorientation, I was able to realize the severity of my situation and felt sincerely grateful to even be alive. I felt personally blessed by God and gave Him endless thanks. At one point, I recall discussions between my physicians and my wife regarding my release from the hospital. While my condition was technically stable, I was still incredibly weak and required heavy doses of medication around the clock. These needs were weighed against the risk of contracting new infections while in the hospital due to my weakened immune system. The doctors suggested admitting me to an inpatient rehabilitation center so I could regain my strength and receive the care I required without being exposed to as many truly sick individuals. I wasn't a huge fan of that plan; I was tired of the hospital, and I just wanted to be back at home. After a bit of persuading, I was able to convince the doctors to discharge me fully under the condition that Louann and I procure daily home nursing care.

So, ready or not, I was coming home. I underwent one final minor surgery to put in two peripherally inserted central catheter (PICC) lines into my right arm and chest. A PICC line is a catheter that gets left in your vein to serve as a direct access point to your bloodstream. The visiting nurses could draw blood from the PICC line and also deliver my intravenous antibiotics through the same tube. It was pretty nice actually, saving me from having to get stuck with needles multiple times a day. After the successful PICC placement, my hospital discharge was on its way to becoming a reality. I was finally able to go home on May 21st, seventeen days after my emergency admission and thirty days since the initial Chiari surgery.

For someone who prided himself on independence and self-sufficiency, my trip home from the hospital ushered in a new modus operandi for our household. My wife took over driving duties in my SUV while our children waited in the driveway to help walk me slowly into the house. I battled conflicting feelings. While I was thankful for my family's assistance, I felt somewhat ashamed and frustrated that I could not walk into my own home unattended. This would be the beginning of my new state of dependence, which I would resent and resist, often to the detriment of our family dynamic. But make no mistake about it, I thanked God for my return home to my family. From a near death experience and a heavenly embrace, I now felt a fresh breeze and the warmth of the sun on my face. A month had already passed since my first surgery, and I was ready to start my path to recovery.

Chapter Sixteen
Home, Antibiotics, and Allergies

The PICC lines were life-savers. Every six hours, the medicine pump attached to the lines would activate and inject life-preserving antibiotics into my bloodstream. If one line became blocked, the doctors had a backup through which to continue the vital treatment. Having only one PICC was too big of a gamble to take. Each time my infusion pump pack kicked on, it made this loud whirring sound that would often startle me awake. The pump was loud, but each time it went off I took comfort in the fact that I was getting the maximum dose of the strongest antibiotics available to combat the bacteria that had taken up residence in my body. The treatment that was prescribed to kill the deadly bacteria was effective, but it carried with it numerous side effects, many of which I would not experience until years later.

Before entering the hospital for the first Chiari surgery in April, I weighed a pretty solid 184 pounds, my approximate weight for the past twenty years of my life. I have always been big into physical conditioning and fitness, pretty much because I needed an outlet to work off the stress from my day job. Running gave me an escape from the daily pressures of work, a time when I could clear my head, focus, and recharge myself. I exercised whenever possible: over lunch breaks, late at night after the kids were asleep, or early in the mornings before meetings. It was almost like therapy for me. I ran three to four miles a day at least five days a week and also participated in a competitive tennis league at least twice a week. I would reward myself occasionally with a donut from the bakery.

When I arrived home after almost a month in the hospital, I weighed 149 pounds and could not walk more than twenty feet without collapsing in exhaustion. I had dropped 35 pounds in a month and went from running miles around my neighborhood to standing hunched over and heavily panting after walking from the living room to the bathroom. The battle my body had undergone while fighting meningitis and sepsis had exhausted me to a point that I never could have imagined. My legs and arms each felt like they weighed a million pounds and my lungs gasped for air as if I was a two-pack-a-day smoker with pneumonia.

At home getting my temperature taken while my infusion pump pack administered antibiotics.

It's startling how much life can change in the blink of an eye. My whole life's direction was diverted so suddenly that I didn't have time to prepare for it. In the months that followed my hospitalization, my priorities became PICC lines and antibiotics, not million-dollar investment portfolios. Instead of discussing holdings and stock strategies with clients, I was discussing white blood cell counts and nausea with my home nurse, Betty. My life had changed.

Betty, as well as a few other nurses, would visit me daily to assess my situation. They repeatedly checked and recorded my vital signs and also drew blood to monitor the levels of infection in my blood stream. The two big things Betty told me to keep an eye on were my white blood cell (WBC) count and my temperature. Together the two readings would give me a pretty good idea of how well my body was fighting off the infection. High WBC counts and high temperatures meant the infection was still raging through my body; conversely, low numbers meant I was headed in the right direction. Each day I'd pray for low WBC counts and low temps, but I could pretty much guess where my numbers would be depending on how I felt that day.

Betty and the nurses came to our house three times a day, every day, for the next three weeks to care for me. I felt like I should have made up the spare bedroom for them; they were practically houseguests. I formed a close bond with all of my caregivers during this period; they saw my moods vary from positive and determined to dispirited and agitated, and they always tried their best to respond accordingly, providing support and guidance, strength and comfort.

After three weeks, it was determined that the medicine pump would be discontinued in favor of manual injections of the medications. The nurse visits became every other day, and only once a day unless I called with a problem. My wife and children were taught how to administer the doses by hand and would be required to inject me with two different vials three times daily. First an IV push of Heparin to thin my blood and keep the PICC line clear and then the injection of the antibiotic Vancomycin. As soon as the medication entered my vein, I could feel an intense chill coursing through my body, tracing the pathway in which the medication was traveling. The chill lasted anywhere from 15 minutes to a full hour, and I often found myself wrapped tightly under blankets, trying to ineffectually ward off the cold. My life revolved around these injections, as I knew that after receiving them, I was sapped of all my energy and rendered useless for at least an hour or so. Some days were worse than others, leaving me exhausted and unable to function for the remainder of the day.

My battle with the infection was a constant emotional rollercoaster. Typically, I love rollercoasters. I'm a big fan of theme parks, and riding the coasters has always been one of my favorite pastimes. But this — this wasn't fun like a theme park at all. The constant stress that accompanied the rise in my WBC counts was nauseating. As soon as the numbers would return elevated, the entire tone in our home would change; we were fearful. When the counts would return to normal, we felt relief, but we also weren't naïve enough to believe that the numbers would stay down. The anxiety was constant.

To make matters worse, I awoke one morning with huge raised red welts that blanketed my entire body. My face was tingly, and my lips were slightly swollen. I have no idea how it happened overnight after taking it for weeks, but I had developed an allergic reaction to the Vancomycin antibiotic. This was particularly troublesome because Penicillin was the only alternate antibiotic left that was capable of eradicating the particular type of bacteria I had, and I had a previous history of allergic reactions to Penicillin and was told by my family doctor that I should avoid it. Granted, I hadn't taken the medicine since I was a child and there was a possibility that I had outgrown the allergy, but this was my absolute last chance. If I was allergic to Penicillin, there would be nothing left to treat me and this infection could kill me. I had little choice but to try it. Each time the medication was injected I said a quick prayer, held my breath, and waited.

I would make it through two full weeks of the Penicillin treatment before developing an allergic reaction to that medication as well. As I only had a few days of treatment remaining, the doctors felt comfortable enough to skip the last couple of doses and hope for the best. After three long months, my prayers had been answered and my body was fully cleared of the Staphylococcus Aureus bacteria that had caused my meningitis infection and septic shock.

Being released from the care of my infectious disease doctor felt like the start of a new chapter. He reiterated how truly lucky I was to have survived the two brain surgeries, bacterial meningitis, and resulting septic shock and early stage organ failure that followed. Statistically, I was an anomaly; according to Dr. Rosario, I probably shouldn't even still be here, yet here I stood. Even though I had survived, the doctors couldn't be sure of what long-term damage had been done, and I was forewarned that problems still could arise down the road. Before Dr. Rosario finally let me go, he shook my hand and gave me some simple advice, "Dale, you're a lucky man who was quite ill. Enjoy your life, make every single moment count." I took his words to heart and awaken every morning recognizing how fortunate I am to be alive and treasuring the joy and beauty each day has to offer.

Chapter Seventeen
Living in Limbo

Without the constant possibility of death looming over me, I was finally able to sit back and assess my situation. My neurologist suggested that I had taken "a pretty big hit" mentally and physically from the illness, but again, he couldn't give me an objective answer regarding what my life would look like from this point forward. I recognized that I currently had some deficits; I was physically weaker, having lost a considerable amount of weight and muscle mass, but I figured I could gain that back in time. My balance was off, and I frequently swayed back and forth as if I had just stepped off a ship in a storm. The left peripheral vision in my left eye had mysteriously vanished, splotches of black filling the lateral fields of my view. Cognitively, I felt a bit slower at mental processing, but it didn't seem to be limiting me too much. *Were these deficits permanent? Was there any chance of improvement or did I just have to learn to live with the deficits?* I needed to devise a plan of attack; I had to get back to work.

Ever since I went in for the first Chiari surgery, there was a clock ticking in the back of my mind regarding my eventual return to work. My job as a financial adviser was demanding and, unfortunately, the financial markets didn't stop simply because I got sick. I was expected to be available for my clients every single day should they require investment advice or stock trades to be placed. It was all about accessibility; each day that I wasn't there to support my clients was a day that they might choose to seek alternate advice, and I couldn't let that happen. My family's financial well-being was wholly dependent on this business that I had built and cultivated over the past 24 years. Without it, I didn't know how I would provide for my family. Remaining out of work was not an option.

My neurologist first wanted to get some baseline testing so we could see where I was. He started with some simple exams like walking heel to toe across the room, touching my finger to my nose, and closing my eyes while trying to maintain my balance. I was almost offended by the simplicity of it all. *The tests sounded so easy.* The difficulty came when I attempted to do them. I couldn't believe how hard it was for me to simply walk in a straight line. As I stepped to place one foot in front of the other, heel to toe, I felt my equilibrium get thrown off, and my entire body lurched violently to the right almost bringing me down to the ground. I tried to overcompensate and leaned strongly to my left, but I somehow ended up in an odd crouching position instead. I couldn't even stand upright with my eyes closed without swaying wildly from side to side. I tried to widen my stance to give myself a greater base of support, which seemed to help a little. Standing with my legs spread wide, I looked like I was consistently preparing to do splits, but it beat the alternative of falling flat on my face.

During the rest of the neurological examination, the doctor noticed that my eyes did not seem to be functioning together properly. Every time my eyes tried to follow his finger I could not keep them focused. He called the condition nystagmus, which forces the eyes to make repetitive uncontrolled movements. That made sense to me; I had been having trouble reading the newspaper lately and felt like I couldn't get my eyes to cooperate and focus together on the page.

Right before leaving the appointment, the neurologist suggested that I see some other specialists for follow up. He referred me to an ophthalmologist to further assess the problems with my eyes as well as a vestibular specialist to see if my inner-ear had any role in my balance issues. I was happy to get the referrals; I craved an understanding as to what ailed me so I could begin to fix the problems at hand. If these issues weren't fixable, it would be okay, but I needed to know so I could start making the necessary adaptations in order to get my life back on track. I felt like I was living in some state of limbo, not knowing at all what my future was going to look like. *Will I get any better? Could I possibly get worse?*

Unfortunately, I knew this limbo feeling all too well. This wasn't the first time my life had taken a detour due to a medical issue. Just when you think you have life all planned out, a completely unplanned event can turn your life in an entirely different direction. Now granted, I was a teenager when the first detour happened, and childhood life plans aren't always realistic, but that doesn't make them any less meaningful at the time.

Ever since I was a kid, I loved playing basketball and dreamed of playing at a Division I University. I remember countless summer evenings spent at the park shooting free throws long after the streetlights had kicked on for the night, hours spent dribbling up and down my street with two balls at a time, criss-crossing them between my legs in rapid succession. I lived for basketball; it was my absolute favorite thing to do. When I was sixteen, my years of practice finally paid off, and I was named a starter on the varsity high school team as a sophomore. I was overjoyed; everything was really looking up for me.

Then, only three weeks into the season, I had a freak accident playing touch football with the neighborhood boys on a Sunday afternoon. I never saw the kid coming; he crashed into me from the side, and I fell onto my right leg, my foot twisting awkwardly as I crumpled to the ground.

I couldn't stand up, and I knew immediately that my ankle was broken. My buddies helped to carry me to a friend's car and got me home to my parents where I tried repeatedly to convince my mother that I was fine, stubbornly refusing to accept that I might have broken my ankle doing something so stupid, especially during basketball season. Basketball was supposed to be my ticket to a prestigious college. My parents didn't earn enough money to send me to an expensive school, and I certainly couldn't save enough myself no matter how many summer jobs I had.

Throughout the night, my ankle swelled significantly and the pain increased in intensity to the point that I could no longer hide its severity from my mother. I cried on and off throughout the night, not so much from the pain but from the utter disappointment I felt from having to miss the basketball season. When I awoke in the morning, my mother drove me to our family physician. Immediately upon seeing me, he directed me to the emergency room, saying, "Son, I don't even have to take an x-ray to know this leg is broken. In fact, it's one of the worst I've seen. Why on earth didn't you go in to the ER last night?" I fought back tears;

even at 16 years old, I knew this freak injury was going to change the entire direction of my life. I wasn't going to be a Division I basketball player after this; I wasn't going to attend a prestigious school or get a scholarship to play basketball. Something as little as a broken ankle just ruined my life's dreams.

I would soon find out the fall broke my tibia, my fibula, and shattered the growth plate between the two bones. It was pretty unsightly; my foot literally pointed straight down, as if it was an extension of my leg. I was told that I might never run the same way again and that one leg might be slightly shorter than the other due to the trauma at the growth plate. The orthopedic doctor said it was "doubtful" that I would be able to make it back before the next season started as I required a significant amount of time in a cast and in physical therapy. I didn't like that answer.

The injury occurred in October, and through hard work and determination I proved the orthopedic doctor wrong and was back playing the next fall, albeit with a significant limp. By the next year, my senior year, I was back to about ninety percent of my previous skill level. I had gotten rid of my limp at that point but was never able to regain my speed or jumping ability. I lost that quick first-step that is so important in basketball. Hundreds of hours of training and a strong sense of optimism got me back almost to where I was, but it unfortunately wasn't good enough to earn me a college scholarship. Regardless, I was proud of what I was able to do to get myself back on the court to play the game that I loved. My mother always instilled in me that hard work and determination can overcome almost any obstacle that is placed in your path.

Because of her, I lived my life fully believing that I could overcome anything in this world if I worked hard and wanted it enough.

I assumed that recovery from bacterial meningitis would be the same, but I soon would discover that some things in life simply cannot be corrected with hard work and determination.

Chapter Eighteen
Assessing the Damage

Without the physical or mental stamina to even make it through a full day at home, there was no chance I could return to my office on a regular basis. The next step on my road to recovery would involve lots and lots of physical therapy (PT).

My first day of outpatient PT would have been pretty comical if it weren't so depressing. I entered the facility all ready to go wearing my favorite workout clothes; I was really excited to start getting myself back into shape. As you might recall, I love fitness and exercising so this place was right up my alley. There were all sorts of free weights, cool looking machines, and people rehabbing every body part from their shoulders all the way down to their toes. My therapist was an incredibly sweet lady named Melanie. She said I was the first patient she'd ever had to survive bacterial meningitis. I told her I was eager to get started so that I could start running again. "Easy there mister," Melanie laughed. "The running will come in time, but we need to start slow. Just trust me and try your best not to get discouraged."

I shrugged, "Okay, I can do that." Melanie handed me two bright pink dumbbells each weighing two pounds. "What the heck do you want me to do with these little things?"

"I want you to curl them." She smiled at me as she said it, knowing that I thought she was totally crazy.

"Sounds good." As I lifted the tiny pink weights once and then twice, my arms began to twitch and shake uncontrollably, wobbling like overcooked pieces of spaghetti. I was so embarrassed. *How did I get so weak this quickly?*

Melanie noticed my frustration and told me that I shouldn't worry; this is exactly how she was expecting our first visit to go. The significant weight loss I experienced plus the long period of time that I was stuck in a hospital bed had completely atrophied my muscles. I had to start over from square one in terms of muscular strength and stamina. "Don't you worry, Dale. Stick with me and I'll have you lifting three pound weights in no time," Melanie said with a chuckle.

A few weeks later after making some strides in PT, I got it in my head that I was going to jog two full laps on a track near my house. I convinced my wife to take me over to the track and run with me, "C'mon Lou, you and me running together; it'll be just like old times." Only it wasn't. I was able to jog with Louann for about 30 steps before having to slow to a walk. After that, I was only able to walk half of one lap before I had to stop and beg my wife to take me home. Louann had to practically carry me back to the car.

After these two events, I quickly began to realize that it would take a great deal of hard work, effort, and faith to help me reach my goal of getting my body back into good physical shape. I would visit with the physical therapist three times a week for the next few months and complete a home program of exercises on my own three times daily. I would also tag along with Louann to the track every chance I could to see if I could make some improvements in my jogging. It took some time, but my first big accomplishment came when I was able to jog an entire lap unassisted. It may not seem like much, but I had tears of joy in my eyes as I crossed the finish line of my first full lap, finally achieving the first goal that I had set for myself physically. Before my illness, I could outrun my wife in a 5K race without difficulty. It would take me a few years before I'd be able to outrun her again.

A week after my first PT visit, I visited the second specialist, the ear nose and throat doctor (ENT)/vestibular specialist. The vestibular system includes parts of the inner ear and brain that help control things like balance and eye movements. With some of the symptoms I had been having, it seemed quite likely that the vestibular system was involved in some way. I underwent some odd tests to assess my hearing and my vestibular functioning. First, I was placed in a dark room with small electrodes taped to the skin around my eyes; the doctor's assistants blew bursts of cold and warm air into my ears while intently watching my eyes for a response to the stimuli. Although strange, the tests yielded some objective results. It was determined that the illness had caused extensive vestibular damage to my left ear as well as thirty percent hearing loss. The vestibular damage was very likely the cause for my balance issues and nystagmus.

I've found that my balance is much better in the daylight because my eyes can somewhat compensate for the vestibular system dysfunction, but at nighttime, when I don't have my vision to help, I have trouble keeping my balance. If I try to walk around at night in an area that isn't well lit, I end up looking like a drunk person staggering home from the bar. On two separate occasions, I've been stopped by the local police while jogging after sunset due to my inability to maintain my balance; both times they thought I was intoxicated. After explaining my situation, they both kindly let me go on my way. I'm thankful they didn't make me do a field sobriety test. I doubt I could have even passed one during the daytime; I definitely would have required a breathalyzer to prove my innocence. Since then, I've discovered that running, or even walking, outside at night is not a good idea for me.

A few years later, a second ENT would also tell me that I shouldn't be running at night. He said that if I absolutely had to be outside during the evening hours, I should purchase a head lamp that I could strap to my forehead like an old coal-miner. *There was no way I was going to buy a head lamp.* I'd rather stumble my way through the dark. He also prescribed something called vestibular therapy, which is like physical therapy but for your balance. After a month of attending regular vestibular therapy sessions, my therapist informed me that there was unfortunately nothing further she could do to help me; the deficits were permanent. The therapist also suggested I acquire a walking stick to carry with me should I have to be outside after dusk. *Nope, not a chance.* My stubborn Dutch pride refused to admit I needed one. Plus, I can only imagine the urban legends people would dream up about a guy who only comes out at night wearing a head lamp and carrying a giant walking stick.

Despite the fact that visits to both the physical therapist and the vestibular specialist didn't yield promising results, I decided to still remain hopeful about my visit to the ophthalmologist. Again, I underwent the usual battery of tests: the classic eye chart, color testing, a colorblindness check, and something called a visual fields test. The visual fields test was meant to measure my entire scope of vision, both central and peripheral. Each eye was measured separately so one eye was blindfolded during each part of the exam. To complete the test, I placed my chin into a chin rest and stared directly ahead into the center of a large white dome. A red light flashed in different locations of the dome and every time I saw the red light go off, I pressed a button that I held in my hand like a Jeopardy buzzer. It seemed simple enough and was even kind of fun at first, but the test lasted forever and became exhausting to my brain and eyes. Even though it was tiring, I felt like I did well.

The doctor came into our examination room with a graphical printout from the visual fields exam. As he placed it down in front of Louann and me, I could see that each circle that represented my eye was completely blackened on the left side, looking almost like a half moon. "Dale, this represents your vision. In particular, the blackened sections illustrate the locations in the circular dome where the red light was projected, but you didn't see it or didn't press your buzzer. Have you noticed any problems seeing things off your left side?"

I would have been lying if I said I hadn't. Ever since I awoke from my second brain surgery, part of my left field of vision was totally blocked out. My left eye seemed to be the worse of the two, my right eye had a lesser degree of blacked out area. The ophthalmologist believed that I suffered brain damage either to the area that processes vision or to the pathway from the eyeball to the brain. I also had developed partial colorblindness and had significant nystagmus in both eyes. He recommended a re-evaluation in three to six months but told me that since the symptoms had already been present for awhile that they likely were going to be permanent.

Three visits to specialists revealed three different hurdles to overcome. I took solace in the fact that I was finally getting some answers regarding the various deficits. At least I knew that there was a reason why I was experiencing these symptoms. For months I had been downplaying the severity of my problems, but seeing on paper the results from the specialists opened my eyes to what I was truly dealing with.

Chapter Nineteen
Growing up Dale

I came into this world kicking and screaming in March of 1957. My mother always liked to joke that I started life off on the wrong foot because I was born with a severely deformed right extremity that bent awkwardly inward at a 90-degree angle. I underwent a corrective surgery as a one week-old baby and then spent six years in a clunky supportive shoe to prevent the clubfoot from turning back inward. Despite its initially grotesque appearance, my foot didn't seem to bother me much and no one treated me any differently because of it. I still roughhoused with my two brothers and ran around with the neighborhood kids, often playing cops and robbers and kick the can until our parents called us home for dinner.

My parents were of Pennsylvania Dutch descent; disciplined, stoic, stubborn, and honest natured. They worked incredibly hard to provide the basic necessities for a household of three active and growing boys. My father was a printer by trade, and my mother helped to make ends meet by working the night shift at the bakery across the street from our home. We often awoke in the morning to the sweet smell of delicious peanut butter buns and chocolate iced doughnuts, still warm and gooey from the oven, that Mom would bring home from the bakery to surprise us. I treasured the mornings when I descended the stairs to find a plain white box tied neatly with twine sitting on the kitchen table. Neither of my parents were the type to express their feelings out loud, but in these moments, I knew that they loved me.

Mom's childhood was particularly rough. From the age of seven until she married my father, she spent her life growing up in an orphanage. Although she rarely spoke of it, I know it affected her deeply. She was a tough cookie, a real disciplinarian who spanked first and asked questions later. She met my father when she was seventeen, and they married a year later. My dad grew up without a father as well, losing his dad to a heart attack when he was only eleven.

My parents' relationship wasn't exactly the picture of an ideal marriage. They fought constantly and our house felt like a war zone, thick with tension and hostility. My brothers and I were often forced to corral ourselves in a bedroom, desperately trying to distract one another from the venomous dialogue that occurred outside of our door. My parents meant well, but their tumultuous relationship cast an ever-present cloud of stress over our household.

Despite their shortcomings, my parents were always present in my life. They taught me right from wrong and brought me up to believe that if I worked hard and was of good moral character that I could be successful in this world.

I started working at a young age, partly to earn some extra spending money and partly because work provided an escape from the hostile environment at home. While some kids my age ran lemonade stands, I dreamed of owning a lawn-mowing business and, at age twelve, decided I was going to start my very own. I borrowed my father's hand-pushed reel mower and went door to door in search of new clients for my business. I negotiated prices, set monthly schedules, hunted down leads and referrals, and then I cut the grass. It was a wonderful learning experience for me because it taught me that in a fee-per-job venture, your success is wholly dependent on how much time, effort, and work you're willing to put into your business. Additional summer jobs ranging from painting, landscaping and hardware store clerk gave me the financial means to see myself through my high school and college years.

Chapter Twenty
Trout and New York

The experiences of my childhood were pivotal in my success as an adult. Upon graduating from college at 22, I was incredibly fortunate to get an interview with the investment firm, Dean Witter, for a job as a financial advisor. During my first interview, I was told immediately that I was far too young for the position. It was 1980 and, at that time, most potential financial advisors were at least in their thirties, boasting years of experience and a solid client referral base from a prior occupation. Despite this obvious shortcoming, I somehow managed to convince the initial interviewer to send me to a second interview with the regional manager in Delaware. I was forewarned that I shouldn't get my hopes up. The manager in Delaware was tough, and he'd likely tell me that I wasn't old enough and lacked proper experience. That didn't bother me; I still had to give it a shot. The worst he could say was, "No."

I soon arrived in Delaware to meet the man I was told I should fear. I nervously sat in his office, my polyester suit irritating the back of my neck, when I happened to catch a glimpse of the stuffed trout adorning his walls. It was at this moment that I realized God was on my side; I had been the president of the fly-fishing club in high school and knew I could use the topic of fishing to find common-ground with a man who was nearly forty years my senior. At the end of our two-hour meeting, he approved me to move on to my final hurdle to clear: the last interview. I was on my way to Dean Witter's corporate headquarters in New York City.

It's over a two hour drive to New York City from where I lived in Eastern Pennsylvania. I spent the entire bus ride trying to re-direct any thoughts of doubt or anxiety into ones of positivity and confidence. I certainly had to believe that I deserved this job before I could win over the executives at Dean Witter. I felt pretty good about my chances, but I was also nervous. As I arrived in Manhattan, I was exhilarated by the sheer liveliness of the city, people hurriedly racing to and fro, cars, bikes, and taxis as far as the eye could see, and tourists snapping photos at every street corner. *I had never seen anything like it.*

Dean Witter's headquarters were housed in the South Tower of the World Trade Center (WTC). Before the interview I took a minute, maybe two, to stand outside of the building, take a good look around and absorb every detail I could about the moment because, if all went well, a snapshot of this day could end up being a defining scene in my life's story. Awed by the size of the World Trade Center, I looked upward trying to gauge how far it stretched into the frigid winter sky. I took one final deep breath and headed inside.

To my surprise, I discovered my nervousness about the inter-view was entirely ill founded; the final interview was simply a for-mality as my previous recommendations were already enough to get me hired. This was more of a "cross our t's, dot our i's" kind of meeting. I was blown away. The executives invited me to a celebratory lunch across the street in the North Tower of the WTC. At this, I immediately became self-conscious again, realizing I would have to leave the building in the middle of a snow shower, and I didn't have a coat. *Well, I did have a coat; it was folded over my left forearm, but it wasn't mine, and it was three sizes too small.* In the business world, appearances are everything, and all the businessmen I knew or had seen before on television wore these heavy wool topcoats in the winter. I didn't want to be seen as someone too poor or too young to own a topcoat so I asked to borrow my Dad's, even though I knew it wouldn't even come close to fitting me. I kept it slung neatly over my forearm, thought warm thoughts, and prayed that no one would notice or ask me about it. Thankfully, no one did.

The restaurant that inhabited the 107th floor at the very top of the WTC was called "Windows on the World," and it was the most exquisite room I'd ever seen with my own eyes. Floor to ceiling windows surrounded me in every direction, and the view was simply otherworldly. I tried not to let the executives I was dining with catch me staring, but I couldn't help but be dazzled by the sight of what looked like a miniature toy city below. It felt as if I was dreaming among the clouds; I was quite literally on top of the world.

I became the youngest financial adviser in the entire country to be hired by Dean Witter at that time. With this distinction came a lot of hard work. My training class started with 54 individuals; three years later, there were only four of us remaining. Many of my colleagues had impressive pedigrees, wealthy business contacts, and diplomas from Ivy League universities. I, unfortunately, possessed none of those things. But what I did have was a relentless work ethic that had been ingrained in me since childhood. My first three years in the business, I worked seven days a week and consistently put my clients first, even before myself or my wife. The early demands of my career and my desire for success are what ultimately led to my unbalanced life.

Chapter Twenty-One
A Long-Delayed Return to the Office

After what felt like an eternity, I finally made my triumphant return to the office, and my work family welcomed me back with open arms. I felt truly blessed to have had a superb staff full of dedicated, smart, and conscientious people who cared for my clients just as much as I did. They all shouldered the burden of my illness and hospitalization, often pulling extra overtime to cover my workload on top of their own.

Prior to developing meningitis, my workdays moved at a frenetic pace. I lived on the telephone, flipping back and forth between different clients on separate phone lines. Early on, I had to learn how to multitask while on the phone with clients; otherwise, I'd never get anything done. It was common for me to be on the phone speaking with one client, while on the computer looking up information for someone else, and simultaneously listening to my assistant update me on the status of the financial markets. Things were hectic to say the least, and my mind was constantly in motion, bouncing from one client to the next, one meeting to another. Luckily, keeping everything straight never seemed to be an issue for me. While other advisers kept meticulous notes to help them remember things, I was always able to recall conversations as if I could replay them back to myself in my mind. It didn't matter if the conversation occurred a week or a year ago, things always seemed to stick in my memory. I wasn't much for physics or mechanical issues, but I was good with recall and numbers.

When I first returned to the office, I tried to limit myself to three to four hours of work each day for three days a week. My self-imposed restrictions didn't last long. By my second week back, I felt mounting pressure to extend my hours because my work load was getting backed up. Clients wanted appointments, new account referrals were piling up in my inbox, and there was a tremendous amount of portfolio review work that needed to be done. Four hours a day was not nearly enough time to accomplish everything. All of this going on while trying to recover physically and mentally was exhausting. It was at this point, as I was trying to get back to my regular work schedule, that I first considered the possibility that I may not be physically capable of returning to the man I once was, the prospect hitting me like a punch to the gut. I'd gone through my entire life believing that I was capable of absolutely anything I put my mind to if I simply worked hard enough. I believed that hard work could overcome all of life's obstacles and that my effort level was the only limiting factor to my success. But now, I couldn't help but wonder, what if I was wrong?

Chapter Twenty-Two
No More Peanut Butter, Please

I couldn't put my finger on it, but something felt off about my cognition. I'd been noticing it for a few weeks; I was so distractible and spacey. I couldn't remain focused on a task or even remember why I was doing things sometimes. I had that feeling when you walk into a room to grab something and then, as soon you get in there, you forget what it was you came in to get. But it felt like a loop, repeating over and over throughout the day. Louann thought I was overloading myself by trying to do too much too quickly. She kindly mentioned, quite a few times, that I should try to slow down and maybe that would help matters. I tried not to let her see me struggle, but I knew she could tell I was having difficulty with complex tasks and with my memory. It must have been difficult for her, caught in the middle and not knowing whether to hold my hand and help me or give me the independence to try things on my own and watch me struggle. She tried desperately to walk this fine line, but often found herself acting like an overbearing parent, trying to shield me from failure and disappointment usually at the expense of my independence. Her concerns about my health were always well-intentioned; she was legitimately worried about the changes she had noticed in my mental abilities, but her constant apprehension and hand-holding was often met on my end by anger and frustration as I continued to vehemently deny that there was anything wrong with me. I was incredibly stubborn and proud, and I needed to prove to my wife that I was capable of regaining my independence without her assistance.

To start, I decided that I would go back to doing the weekly grocery shopping on my own, as Louann and I had been doing this task together since my illness. Grocery stores were a dangerous place for me, their aisles littered with advertisements for sales, colorful displays, and a multitude of different products with similar packaging. All of this was too much stimulation for my brain to handle, and I'd end up wandering down the aisles, distracted and confused while trying to calculate the best deal or remember what brand of dish soap we used to buy. What used to be a twenty minute trip to the store now took me close to two hours and, for some odd reason, I'd always come home with a jar of peanut butter thinking we were out of it. Louann was surprisingly understanding about it, adding each new jar to the cabinet until we had shelves and shelves of peanut butter. After I had stocked the cabinet full of every possible variety of Skippy and Jif, Louann kindly suggested that I may benefit from the use of a shopping list. At the top of the list each week in giant red letters she would write the words, "NO PEANUT BUTTER." I think to this day, none of my family members will willingly eat a peanut butter and jelly sandwich, having tired of them years ago while attempting to consume all the peanut butter I'd bring home from my grocery trips.

Everything I attempted to do seemed to take longer. Often, I wasn't able to even complete tasks I set out to accomplish. My foolish pride made it difficult for me to let anyone know that I was having issues; I refused to believe that there were certain things that I couldn't overcome by just working through them.

One day, however, the truth hit me in the face like a ton of bricks. I was in my office when my operations manager came down to see me. Linda worked at the firm since my date of hire back in 1980, and we'd become pretty close friends over the twenty or so years we'd known each other. As soon as she walked in, I could tell something was wrong just by the look on her face. She informed me that I had made a pretty significant trading error for one of my clients that ended up costing a few thousand dollars. In the finance world, a trading error that was made by you was paid by you, so screwing up could cost you a fair amount of money out of pocket. There was no such thing as malpractice insurance for financial advisors to protect against human error. Prior to my surgery, I had made one or two trading errors over the course of my career, but an error had never cost me more than a few hundred dollars. This error was a sizable one, and it occurred only a few weeks after my return to work, which had me worried. Having to pay the few thousand dollars bothered me a little, but the scariest thing was that I didn't even remember placing the trade order. I had a real dilemma on my hands. Jars of peanut butter aside, my cognition was now negatively affecting my clients and destroying the trust they had placed in me. The error brought to light what I had been desperately trying to ignore: I was no longer able to do my job successfully.

Chapter Twenty-Three
Labeled Disabled

One rainy September morning, my office manager stopped by unexpectedly for a closed-door meeting. He pulled a chair up to my desk and spoke calmly yet firmly, "Dale, we're all worried about you. Your assistants have previously approached me with concerns regarding your health but, after the trading error, I had to officially notify corporate. I have to tell you, they want you to undergo some testing just to make certain you're okay." It just so happened that just a few days earlier my neurologist had suggested I pay a visit to a neuropsychologist.

I went to get tested to satisfy the firm as well as myself. The exams were designed to assess various aspects of my cognition including memory, recall, verbal abilities, vocabulary, reasoning skills, arithmetic, and language comprehension, all things necessary to perform my job sufficiently. Some tests were verbal while others required paper and pencil. They all seemed simple and straightforward enough, yet confusing and tiring at times.

I was told after the fact that the testing was designed to be finished in one day, but it took me a day and a half. Despite the tests taking me so long, I felt like I had performed well on them, and

I was excited to get the results and prove to everyone that I was okay. Louann and I had an agreement that if I scored normally on the exams, I would return to my job full-time, provided my firm would allow it. If I did poorly on the testing, I would accept my fate and move on.

The follow up appointment with the neuropsychologist was the next day to review my results. As I entered his office, I couldn't help but feel a little nervous. *I truly felt like I had passed the exams with flying colors, but what if I hadn't? Would I really have to quit my career?* In the past, my work had taken up so much of my time and effort that being a financial adviser became a large part of my personal identity. *If I didn't get to be a financial adviser anymore, who was I?* I quickly pushed the self-doubt out of my mind. Ever since I was a little kid, I've had a tendency towards optimism regarding my life and generally believe that things will always end up okay in the end. *I mean, why would I torture myself by thinking otherwise?*

Walt Disney once said, "I always like to look on the optimistic side of life, but I am realistic enough to know that life is complex." At this moment, I was certainly finding life to be complex, but I still felt confident in a positive outcome. Now I just needed the doctor to confirm that I was good to go back to work, and I'd be able to look back at this testing as just a small bump in the road on my life's journey.

The appointment started quite well. The doctor explained my over-learned skills such as word recognition, spelling, and arithmetic were at a level consistent to before my illness. In other words, I was as smart, or as dumb, as I was before the illness. *Whew, that was a relief!* However, he told me that I had taken a "hit" which had impaired my ability to process information. On several neuropsy-chological measures my scores had taken a complete nosedive. My comprehensive memory test was ranked in the lowest fifth per-centile for my age group, significantly below my premorbid level. The doctor carefully explained that, although my intelligence re-mained fully intact, my ability to process information was severely impaired, making it difficult for me to think, react, and remember as quickly as I did before. He said, "Given the nature of your oc-cupation and the necessity to function at a highly efficient level, I find that you are not capable of performing the tasks required of your current job."

I glanced to my left towards Louann and saw tears streaming profusely down both cheeks. She immediately realized how much this news would affect both of our lives going forward. Predict-ably, it took me far longer to understand the full impact of the results. This neuropsychologist held my entire career and future in his hands. I had overcome physical obstacles in the past, but I didn't know how to fix my brain. *Was it even possible?* Given the results of my testing the neuropsychologist advised that I should begin the application process for disability.

The weight of the doctor's words came crashing down around me and, for the first time since my mother died, I wept. The rev-elation that I was no longer the man I thought I was felt life-shat-tering. *Surely the tests were wrong? Would they let me retake them?* I felt good about my performance and figured this had to be some sort of mistake. I had promised Louann that I would accept the results of the test regardless of the outcome, but I never expected this. I was in no way ready to leave my profession of twenty-four years.

This wasn't right; I was only forty-six years old, nowhere near retirement age. I had so much left to accomplish and so much more to offer to my clients.

Leaving the doctor's office that day, I knew that my life had changed forever. The front office in New York would never let me go back to my old position as they could not take on the legal risks that my substandard test results had presented. For the past twenty-four years I had given so much of myself to my occupation that I had allowed my job to fully define my personal identity. I was Dale Reppert, Financial Adviser. *I didn't know how to be anything else.* So much of my self-worth was tied to my success in my career that I began to lose track of who I was. *How could I ever be successful again if I wasn't gainfully employed? Was there a way to adjust my definition of success for my life going forward?* Luckily for me, I would soon discover that God closes doors for a reason and that there are far better things ahead than what we leave behind.

Chapter Twenty-Four
My Reluctant Retirement

My last day of work was an unseasonably warm day in October. It was not how I expected my career to end. There was no fanfare, no retirement party, just me and a few boxes for my belongings. Cleaning out my office was no easy task; over the past twenty-four years I had accumulated a substantial amount of photographs and memorabilia, each carrying with it a special memory from a better time. There was a photo from the set of the local television program I hosted on PBS for two years called, "Insights to Investing." I loved hosting that show and connecting with callers from all over the tri-state area. The show provided great publicity for my firm and me, and Louann reveled in the fact that I was a local celebrity, playfully chiding me whenever someone would approach me and say, "Hey, aren't you that guy from…"

One of my first days on the set of "Insights to Investing" which aired locally on PBS

I boxed up the plaques from my inductions into the President's and the Director's Clubs, remembering just how proud I was to have earned my place among some of the best and brightest in the entire company. My eyes turned their focus to the pictures of Louann and my children sitting proudly upon my desk. I had placed them right next to my computer screens to serve as a constant reminder of exactly why I was working so hard. My family was the ultimate reason I threw myself into the business; I wanted desperately to provide for them, to give them a life that I never had. When it came time to pack away the two picture frames from my desk, I was overcome with emotion and had to ask my staff to step out of the room for a few minutes. For the second time in less than two months, I broke into tears. Silent tears quickly progressed into sobs as my head fell into my hands. *How am I going to provide for my family now? What are we going to do?* Taking one last look around the bare walls of my office, I couldn't help but feel defeated. I was grateful to be alive, but was ashamed at what had become of me; I felt like I had failed and let my entire family down.

Chapter Twenty-Five
A Second Chance

It is said that when God closes one door, he opens another. I wholeheartedly believe that today, but back in 2004, I needed some convincing. After being forced into early retirement from Morgan Stanley, I kept banging on the door that God had closed by obsessively coveting my old job and my old life. I wasted so many days in a state of denial, unwilling to let go of my old life and failing to see the beauty in what I had been given: a second chance.

Louann suggested that I remain busy and focus on the things that I could still do rather than the one thing that I couldn't. One day when I was feeling particularly low, she said something that really resonated with me, "There are so many other ways to help people besides managing their money." She was right. For so long, I tied my self-worth to my ability to help my clients that I neglected to see the myriad of other ways that I could still be helping people.

I returned to my position on the school board. I had zero plans of re-running for the seat but, while I was in the hospital, the local community began a write-in campaign for my re-election. That fall I was elected for not one, but two, positions by write-in vote: School Board Member and County Constable. The local paper even did a story on me because I was the first person in the history of the county to be elected to two positions by a write-in vote. I accepted the school board seat but declined the constable position. *For one, I had no idea what a constable even did.* I later found out that they serve subpoenas, transport criminals, and protect the peace in their communities. They even can arrest people and carry a badge and a firearm. While I was honored by the election, I certainly did not think it was wise to let a guy with balance problems, poor vision, a lousy memory, and snail-like reaction time to carry a gun. *Could you imagine?* I'd be the worst constable in the history of Pennsylvania, stumbling around at night trying to execute an arrest warrant with my badge, gun, walking stick, and coal-miner headlamp.

Being retired/disabled also gave me the ability to seek out experiences that I previously never would have had the time to undertake. I was able to get more involved at my church by serving as a Deacon for the next six years, which was the maximum term limit at the time. There I attended consistory meetings, headed up the financial committee, and acted as an usher during church services. Those six years helped to form connections with other Christians in my community that were ultimately vital to my spiritual growth.

Just as iron sharpens iron, so one man sharpens another. ~ Proverbs 27:17 KJV

Through my contact and fellowship with my newly discovered church family, my own rough edges were beginning to become smoother; I was learning patience, kindness, tolerance, and love. By being exposed to various points of view and to different feelings and values, I grew in my understanding of the Bible, the Christian way of life, and how God works in the lives of others. I learned to fill the void of pride from my success at work with satisfaction that I derived from helping other people.

Chapter Twenty-Six
Disability Realization

Once my test results became available to my firm, it was officially requested that I apply for disability benefits. Thankfully, I had the foresight to purchase three disability policies dating back to the 1980's in case a situation should arise where I was incapacitated and unable to continue working. My wife was thrilled to discover that these policies would supply approximately 50% of our prior year's income, tax free. These disability payments would continue throughout our lifetime, supplying us with enough money to survive. I recall feeling relief that our family would be receiving income despite my inability to work, but it also forced me to face the stark reality that there was more wrong with me than I was willing to admit.

Had I not carried personal disability insurance, the added stress it would have put on me and my family would have been devastating. Worrying about paying bills while attempting to recover physically, mentally, and emotionally would have been very challenging, to say the least. I had always carried life insurance coverage that would allow my wife and family to live comfortably in the event of my untimely death, but disability coverage was often harder to justify spending my money on. *I figured, Hey, I'm young and healthy, I don't smoke or drink—what's the worst that could happen?* If I hadn't carried disability coverage, I would have been forced to tell my wife that not only would she now have to care for me physically, but she'd also have to find a way to support our family financially as well. That alone would have crushed me.

My disability policy had a subrogation clause stating that I also had to apply for Social Security Disability. If I were to be approved for Social Security, any payments they made would be deducted from my private disability payments. This process required multiple examinations from numerous physicians who worked on behalf of the Social Security department. I remember stubbornly telling each doctor that I was fine and that I didn't think I truly qualified for disability benefits. While I knew I couldn't do the primary tasks of my old position as a financial adviser, I certainly could work elsewhere, procuring a simpler type of work. I wholeheartedly assumed that I would be rejected from Social Security benefits. I had heard that it was very difficult to be approved on your first application, plus I pretty much told every physician I encountered that I felt I was capable of working in some capacity. *I didn't want to be on disability.* To my surprise, I was notified by mail a short time later that my benefits had been approved, thus deeming me unfit for even menial work.

My detour to heaven became a detour for my entire life. I went from being a high-level financial executive to being someone the federal government believed was not qualified to do any type of work. Being labeled disabled was a severe hit to the reality of who I thought I was, but my thoughts and reality began to change from that point forward. I started to realize that God had detoured my life for another purpose, one not meant for finances and investments. While I took a hit from the meningitis, I had gained a new perspective which has led me to live a more fulfilling life than I would have ever thought possible.

In this world you will have tribulation; but be of good cheer; I have overcome the world. ~ John 16:33 KJV

Acknowledging my disability could have led me down a never-ending road of despair, pain and suffering, but as John Chapter 16, Verse 33 tells us, I decided to turn towards God and be of good cheer. I would not live my life feeling sorry for myself. Disability or not, I was not going to waste what precious time I had left in this wonderful world.

Chapter Twenty-Seven
Louann: Changes in Dale

Thanksgiving was upon us, and we were so incredibly fortunate and thankful to have the entire family together for the holiday. Dale seemed excited to have everyone here, as it was just over four weeks ago that he had been relieved of his job. Over the past few months, I had been noticing the physical and mental impairments that my husband had suffered due to his illness. He tried his hardest not to let the children and me see him struggle, but I could clearly see that things were changing. We pretended that everything would return back to normal to spare Dale's feelings, but the more time that passed, the more I realized that this was our new normal. There was no going back.

Upon removing the turkey from the oven, we all sat down around the dining room table. Per family tradition, we go around the table each year to give thanks to God and to recognize and pray for the things we are most thankful for. Dale usually goes first, but this year, I figured I'd start. With tears welling in my eyes, I thanked God for bringing Dale back home to me and for keeping our family whole. One by one, everyone at the table joined in, thanking God and sobbing uncontrollably. We knew in our hearts that although Dale was different, we were truly blessed to have him home.

In December, we decided to take a trip to Disney World to vacation with Dale's younger brother Todd and his family. Todd lived in Texas so it was the first time that he had seen Dale since his illness. I figured that it would do my husband some good to take a vacation and spend some time with his brother in Disney World since it has always been our family's favorite vacation spot. Also, it was important for Dale to be in familiar surroundings, and he knew Disney like the back of his hand.

The journey to Orlando was an adventure. The flight messed with Dale's vestibular system and left him staggering and unsteady for the rest of the day. He was unable to stand upright, and every step he took left the impression that he was about to tumble over, his left arm wobbling back and forth in an attempt to maintain his balance. I suggested we sit down to eat something at the airport, hoping that a little time spent on stable ground would resolve his equilibrium issues. As usual, Dale insisted that he stand in line to get the food while I looked for a table. Before I knew it, five minutes turned into ten while I remained at the table waiting for my husband. I overheard a man nearby tell his wife, "Sorry it took so long. The restaurant employee asked this guy in front of me what he wanted and the guy just stared off into space like an idiot." I immediately knew he was talking about Dale. I felt my face flush with anger, and I was just about to say something when I saw Dale walking towards me, awkwardly balancing a tray of food in his arms with a lopsided grin on his face. I quickly composed myself; I couldn't let what other people said bother me or ruin our trip. I loved this man and admired the way he fought to get back home to us. It was just so frustrating to see how other people were treating him now. People pointed and stared at him in the airport as he was staggering down the jetway. They probably assumed he had a little too much to drink on the flight. After seeing Dale struggling to remain upright in the lobby, the hotel staff assigned us a disability room even though we didn't request one. Todd had yet to see Dale like this and seemed a bit taken aback by the changes in his brother, "Has it always been this bad?" he asked.

I had told Todd about what things were like at home, but I guess things didn't really sink in until he saw it with his own eyes.

As the new year began, I took notice of a visible change in my husband's personality. In the past, Dale was always the steady provider in our household. He was our protector, doing his best to insulate us from any pain or misfortune. However, after his illness, it felt as if our roles had reversed and I became very protective of him. It felt as if, in some ways, I had another child in the house to take care of. It was difficult for me to allow him the independence he craved because I wanted to protect him from failure. I knew Dale wasn't the same, and I couldn't stand to watch him struggle and flounder. There was a constant conflict between us because he continued to be in denial that anything was wrong with him, even when all objective testing said otherwise. I continually asked if he needed help and he would always say no; *but I knew that he did need my help, he was just too ashamed to admit it.* I hated having to tell him that I didn't think he was capable of doing certain things by himself, but it felt like he was in need of a serious reality check. When he told me he wanted to start going grocery shopping on his own, I told him that I didn't think it was a good idea. He went off on his own for a few minutes to grab some things at Walmart one time and ended up getting so turned around that I had to have him paged over the public address system over an hour later. When the Walmart employee brought him back up to the front of the store, he looked stunned, like he had no idea where he'd been for the past hour. There were just certain things that weren't safe for him to do on his own anymore, but when I tried to address this with him, he would become furious with me. My husband, who prior to this hardly ever got upset or even mildly annoyed, was now having episodes of rage unlike anything I had ever seen in him. Eventually the episodes became more frequent, and I was forced to confront the changes in Dale.

We began seeing a psychiatrist together hoping to help one another work through the frustration and the changes we both were experiencing. The psychiatrist believed Dale was suffering from a mild form of intermittent explosive disorder, where he was experiencing outbursts of anger that were disproportionate to the situations at hand. The neurologist had previously explained the possibility that Dale's brain chemistry had been altered by the meningitis which could have led to this problem. I tried my best to handle the outbursts, believing that he wasn't purposefully lashing out at me or the children, but one summer day, I witnessed Dale punch our son in the arm while screaming at him over some insignificant tennis practice drill. It was then I knew I needed to make a change.

As hard as it was, I decided to take Tyler, our one child who was not in college at the time, to Florida to enroll in a tennis academy. I couldn't risk my son's or my own emotional and physical health to these uncontrollable outbursts. I hoped that if Tyler and I left for a while, Dale could have the independence he desired plus some time alone to recapture the man he was deep inside before all of this happened. It was the hardest decision of my life, yet I felt backed into a corner as if I had no other choice. I loved my husband dearly, and I knew he still loved me, but we needed some time apart.

During the months I lived in Florida, Dale and I would still visit each other often, and we spoke daily on the phone. I was still his biggest supporter, but it seemed like the best thing I could do to help him was to give him the space and independence he craved. With Dale, I felt like my constant worrying and desire to assist him was only hindering his recovery. He needed and wanted to do this on his own so I let him. It ended up being one of the best decisions I've ever made. The time spent apart gave Dale a chance to develop his independence without worrying about letting his family see him struggle. He was too proud to risk failure in front of us so he'd often put on a performance, acting as though nothing was wrong and purposefully avoiding tasks that he may not succeed at on the first try. Without us around, he was free to develop more difficult skills, to try things that were out of his comfort zone and to fail without having to worry about his pride. God answered our prayers, and slowly but surely Dale was able to find inside of him the mild tempered man whom I had married many years ago.

Chapter Twenty-Eight
Tennis with the Guys

Tyler leaving for Florida was not something that blindsided me. Louann and I had previously kicked around the idea of enrolling him at Saddlebrook Preparatory School even prior to my becoming sick. He had shown great promise in tennis and, even as a lanky teenager, he was getting some looks from college coaches. The one thing that did surprise me, however, was that my wife chose to accompany him. I'd been aware that things in our home were difficult, but I never once expected my wife to leave. For the first time in decades, my house was empty, and I woke up alone.

I struggled with my newfound freedom at first, unsure of what exactly to do with myself. I tried to develop a daily routine to help adjust to life alone. I'd wake up, feed the cats, watch a financial news program on TV, eat some cereal, read the paper, and then glance expectantly up at the clock only to be disappointed. *10:30 am? Really, that's it? What else can I possibly do today?* I missed my wife, and I missed the kids. I spent a lot of time talking to my family by phone each day, sometimes even inventing random reasons to call my wife, besides the brutally obvious reason that I missed her voice. "Hey Lou, what kind of detergent do we use in the washing machine?" I'd bother her in Florida, often keeping her on the line for hours just to see how her day was going or to discuss how Tyler was doing in school.

One day out of the blue I received a phone call from a friend who lived nearby. He mentioned that a few of his buddies were getting together for a game of doubles tennis and asked if I would like to join them. Up until that phone call, I hadn't even picked up a tennis racket knowing the outcome would likely be embarrassing and frustrating. I had asked some of my physicians if I would be physically able to play due to my balance and eye issues, and I was told it probably wasn't the best idea. They recommended golf as a safer alternative because the ball doesn't move and you get to ride in a cart instead of having to walk. But being one to never listen to what people told me I couldn't do, I accepted my friend's doubles invitation. *And I'm so glad that I did.*

The gentlemen that I played with were about ten to twenty years older than I was, but they were in great physical condition and were very capable tennis players. That's one of the things I love about the sport, you can play tennis your entire life and continue to be competitive at it as you age. My tennis friends welcomed me to their game with open arms and, to my amazement, I was somehow able to hang with them. I owe a great deal to these guys for allowing me to gain back some of the self esteem I'd been so sorely missing. *If I could play tennis, what else might I be able to do?* Of course, it took some time for me to shake the rust off, but with each match I felt better and better. I would never quite be the same player I was prior to my illness, but that didn't matter; I was enjoying the game and the companionship that it provided. I have thanked these gentlemen many times over the years for providing me with a boost of self-confidence at a time when I needed it the most.

Eventually, I began hosting these tennis matches weekly at the tennis court behind my house. We had a court built in our backyard when the kids were younger because all of our family members are avid tennis players. We put it to good use, too. Some of my favorite family memories took place on that court, from teaching the kids how to swing a racket through the first time they beat Louann and me in doubles. We consider the money truly well spent as our court has hosted thousands of hours of tennis, not only for our family but for a multitude of local tennis players as well.

Since my illness, I've taken a particular interest in promoting the game of tennis in our area. My wife and I have found a way to give back to our community by providing countless hours of free lessons to children of all ages, backgrounds, and ability levels. We have tried to make the game more accessible by donating rackets, shoes, and tennis balls to many of the children we've encountered. Louann and I have taken great satisfaction in helping these children further their lives through the great game of tennis. We attempt to not only teach the sport but also to incorporate important life lessons regarding discipline, self esteem, and work ethic along the way.

As funny as it may sound, the game of tennis helped me to feel normal again. The guys I played with and the children I taught never once looked at me as if I was disabled; I was just Dale, and it felt really good to be that guy again.

My tennis buddies and me (second from the right)

Chapter Twenty-Nine
Louann: One Last Test

After my return from Florida, Dale was doing better and finally coming to grips with his new life as a disabled individual. *Or at least that's what I had thought.* A few years had passed since the original neuropsychological testing, and I figured that chapter of our lives was past us. *You know the one where Dale denies his disability and I have to be the evil, yet reasonable one that brings him back down to earth.* But I was wrong; it wasn't past us just yet.

Dale mentioned to me one morning at breakfast that he was thinking of having himself re-tested cognitively so he could try to get his old job back. He dropped the idea into the conversation so casually, like it wasn't this big huge deal that carried with it significant consequences for both of us as well as our children. I was very apprehensive and, frankly, quite angry with my husband. *We were able to live comfortably on the disability payments from Dale's policies. Was he really willing to give them up and risk the financial security of our family just because he was too proud to consider himself disabled?* I let him know that I didn't approve of the idea, reminding him that he still experienced significant difficulties when he had to focus on more than one task at a time. We argued and argued until I offered to call the neuropsychologist to set up a consultation. *Let's let him tell you that you are not capable of returning to your old job; I'm tired of being the bad guy.* I scheduled an appointment with the original doctor who determined Dale was unfit to return to work, hoping again he could talk some sense into my husband and get him to move on once and for all, knowing all too well that sometimes it helps to hear it from someone else.

We met Dr. Deterk in the same office as we had years earlier, and Dale wasted no time in stating his case, "Despite what Louann may have told you, I am aware that I have some shortcomings, but I feel like I've made some incredible improvements since the last time I was tested, and I'd just like to see where I stand."

He looked over at me, and I could finally see the pain in his eyes, "If the results are similar to last time, I promise you that I'll accept my inability to work; but honestly Lou—I feel guilty; I'm getting this money every month that I haven't earned. Maybe I can't go all the way back to being a financial adviser again, but there's got to be at least something that I can do to provide for my family."

At long last, I was able to get to the true root of my husband's insistence on returning to work. It wasn't just that he loved his job or that he derived self-worth from his prominent position in society. In the end, my husband simply valued the ideal of working for a living and providing for his family. At this discovery, there was no way I could say no to the testing. If Dale wanted to work, then that's what he was going to do; I couldn't take that away from him. If worse came to worse, I'd get a job or the kids could help out. *We'd find a way to manage. We always did.*

The results of the testing returned within a day. Dale said he felt cautiously optimistic that he did well on the exams. *He'd always say that though; I'd never met anyone who was more optimistic in their abilities than Dale.* As Dr. Deterk entered the room, I reached for Dale's hand, prepared to accept the test results whichever way things ended up. Sadly as I had expected, Dale's test results showed no improvement. Overall, the test results were worse than his previous performance. He explained that Dale's ability to process information was irreparably damaged and therefore he did not have the ability to perform the tasks of his old position. His recommendation was unchanged: full disability, incapable of maintaining a full or part time job.

Dale took the news particularly hard. A small part of him had always been holding out hope that, maybe one day, he'd improve and be able to contribute to society again. Deep down I knew that he didn't have a chance of passing. I witnessed his shortcomings and deficiencies daily and was brutally aware of the things my husband could and could not do. Still, my heart broke for him, knowing he finally would have to give up his idea of providing for our family.

Chapter Thirty
My Wake-Up Call

It is often said that God speaks to us in many different ways, but we have to open our eyes and hearts to hear him. When it came to my spirituality, I was always a slow learner, not realizing what God had intended for me until it practically smacked me square in the nose. Over the past few years, I've come to believe that God has been asking me to share my story with others, but it took another alarming wake-up call for me to finally realize my purpose.

Ever since my bout with meningitis, I have maintained annual visits with my neurosurgeon so he can keep tabs on me and make sure I remain healthy. At the most recent visit, I made mention that my gait and balance had been worsening and I'd been having more frequent headaches with some episodes of facial and hand numbness. It had been awhile since my last imaging study so the doctor ordered an MRI of my brain to check things out. In addition he decided to order an MRA, which I hadn't had for quite a few years. The MRI looks at the entire brain, and the MRA more specifically focuses on the blood vessels inside the brain. While I knew this testing was likely coming, I hated the idea of having to do another MRI. It was quite an unnerving experience; having my head strapped down in an enclosed tube terrified me. Thankfully, my wife sat with me at the end of the machine for the full 90 minutes, resting her hand on my leg and repeatedly assuring me that I would be okay.

The testing was performed on a Wednesday, and I was scheduled for a follow up appointment two weeks later to go over the results. Having had my fair share of medical scares throughout my lifetime, I've learned that it's typically not a good sign if the physician calls personally after a test he has ordered; it's an even worse sign if he calls immediately after the test. Sometimes no news is the best news, but a phone call within a day or two from the ordering physician tends to be a pretty bad omen. Upon getting my call the next day from Dr. Deterk, I recognized that my scans were likely abnormal. Another thing I've noticed over the years was that doctors don't like to tell their patients bad news over the phone; they will instead schedule a follow up visit so they can share the news in person. While I appreciate the face-to-face time, the days of uncertainty prior to the appointment are enough to drive anyone crazy. On the phone, I was told that my MRA showed some irregularities and that my results were handed over to the Stroke Division of the Neurosurgical Department. At first, I was confused. *Wait, you're giving me to a different Doctor? Why?* I was told that the arterial irregularity was something that he did not specialize in, and he felt that there was someone more qualified to handle my case. I hung up the phone, and immediately though of my wife who had been through so much already; I couldn't stand the thought of having to bring her more bad news. Rather than be truthful and brave, I fibbed and told her that my doctor suggested that one of his colleagues review my case as a second opinion. I felt terrible lying to my wife, but I was also getting tired of breaking her heart with every doctor's appointment, hospital stay, and imaging result. *She didn't sign up for this.*

As we drove to the doctor's office, we passed Hershey Park and the old Chocolate Factory. I longed for the days when trips to Hershey meant smelling chocolate in the air, eating giant cupcakes, and riding rollercoasters until we felt sick. Today, I felt sick for an entirely different reason, the pit of my stomach balled up in large knots. I began to feel guilty about not telling my wife the true reason for our visit, but I still held out hope that maybe everything would be okay.

The nurse called my name, and Louann and I headed back into the patient area where I began my usual light-hearted banter with the nursing staff. I tend to make small talk when I get nervous, a tic that my wife playfully pointed out during one of our previous doctor's visits. We were brought back to an exam room with eggshell white walls, two navy-blue plastic chairs, and an examining table. A poster of the brain adorned the wall to my right, and there was a detailed map of the brain's circulation to my left. I spent a minute gazing at the circulation map. *Somewhere in here there's an irregularity, huh?* My eyes started to go blurry as I tried to visually follow all of the various tributaries from each of the major arteries. It all seemed so complex and amazing, the way that we are put together anatomically truly a wonder to behold. Finally, I grabbed the seat next to my wife and began to wait. I normally don't sweat much, but for some reason, I was perspiring as I waited for the doctor. The room was so silent that the clock's audible ticking became almost deafening, each second bringing with it greater and greater levels of anxiety. Thankfully, the wait wasn't long, and the ticks were interrupted by three quick sharp knocks at the door. Dr. Barrons kindly introduced himself as the head of the neurosurgery stroke center and then asked us if we would be comfortable if a few of his colleagues joined us in the room. I gave a nod of approval and the door swung open to reveal a small group of white-coated doctors. Two of them appeared to be older, well-established neurosurgeons while the others were much younger, likely residents or fellow physicians who were practicing under Dr. Barrons.

As the additional staff entered the room, I turned my attention back to Dr. Barrons, who, to my surprise, had already pulled up my MRA on the computer screen. I hesitantly glanced in Louann's direction, knowing that at this point she probably had realized that this wasn't just a second opinion. She looked at me, bewildered, and mouthed "What is this?" The look on her face nearly broke my heart into a million pieces.

I reached for her hand, and we both turned our attention back to Dr. Barrons as he began to speak, "Mr. and Mrs. Reppert, I've invited other members of my staff here today because, to be honest with you, I'm a bit confused by your scans. The reason I'm so confused is that whenever we see an MRA result that looks like yours, the patient is typically really bad off."

"Well, how bad off are we talking?" Louann asked wearily.

"They are usually dead, Mrs. Reppert, or at least paralyzed to some degree. Certainly not walking, talking, or functioning like your husband is currently. Dale's case is quite unusual; I've actually never seen anything like it, and neither have my colleagues."

Dr. Barrons turned towards his map of the brain's circulation and used his pen to trace over a large branch, "Do you see this artery right here? This is the Middle Cerebral Artery or MCA, and it is one of the three major arteries that supply your brain. You have one of these on each side. Now, remember how this looks on the wall because we're going to take a look at your images now."

It didn't take a radiologist to recognize that mine looked markedly different. Where the map's MCA was long and had many finger-like projections spiraling out towards the edges of the brain, my MCA was practically non-existent. In its place was an empty space. "Uh, so where's the rest of it?" I asked. "That one side doesn't seem to look anything like the other one. They should look more symmetrical, right?"

"Exactly, so on the right side of your brain, your MCA is narrowed by about 50% but you are still able to get enough blood flow through to perfuse the areas of the brain distal to the blockage."

"So you're saying it's kind of like a hose with a small kink in it." I said, trying to normalize it into something Louann and I could more easily comprehend. "Not as much water gets through after the hose is kinked but you still get enough through to water the garden."

"That's right, perfect," Dr. Barrons continued. "Ok, now on the left side of your brain, the MCA is 100% occluded which has caused those portions of the artery distal to the blockage to essentially just shrivel up and die off. So, going back to your garden hose analogy, it would be like putting a clamp on the hose so that no water was able to get through, and, you know after a while, the far end of the hose that hasn't been able to get water, the garden dries up."

At this, I could see Louann tearing up. But, I was still confused, "Doctor, I understand what you're saying but if that MCA is completely blocked, why am I not dead or paralyzed? People have strokes if they don't get blood flow to their brain, right? Isn't that what a stroke is?"

"Yes it is. And by your test results, I have to assume that at some point in your life you suffered a major stroke. Miraculously, your body has compensated to some degree by generating small collateral blood vessels in an attempt to bypass the blockage. Now, this is by no means the optimum way for blood to be delivered to that area of the brain, but right now it's doing the job well enough to keep you alive." He looked down at his shoes for a moment and then slowly brought his gaze upward until his eyes met mine, "You're a lucky man, Mr. Reppert, but you're living on borrowed time." He proceeded to tell me to enjoy my life, that he couldn't tell me how long the collaterals would hold up. Currently the blood flow was adequate, but for how long he couldn't answer.

Before we left the office, my wife asked one of the neurosurgeons if there was a surgical way to relieve the blockage. Unfortunately, surgery was not an option in my case. The condition in my brain was already so tenuous that no surgeon would risk performing surgery, the results most certainly being paralysis or death.

It was on this day that I finally was given the courage to share the story of my detour to Heaven with anyone who would listen. My wife, family, and friends had been on my case for years trying to get me to share my story by writing a book, but I was always reluctant; my experience felt so personal, and I wasn't sure if anyone would even care. *I mean, who was I to tell people how to live their lives? Why would anyone give a hoot about what I saw?* But then, after this appointment, I recognized that I shouldn't even be alive right now and that there had to be a greater reason why God was choosing to keep me around. Sharing my story was always something I had thought about, and it finally felt like the right time to do so. I figured that if even one person was able to find solace in my depiction of Heaven, that I owed it to them to share my story. When times get hopeless and we are filled with despair, I hope we can find comfort in the fact that a place of perfect peace is awaiting us in God's kingdom.

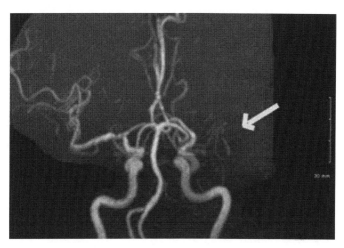

Pictured above: Dale's MRA with the arrow indicating the area of occlusion in the distribution of the Middle Cerebral Artery. Typically, both sides of the study should be nearly symmetrical mirror images of one another. Dale's MCA on the left in this image obviously appears quite different from his MCA on the right.

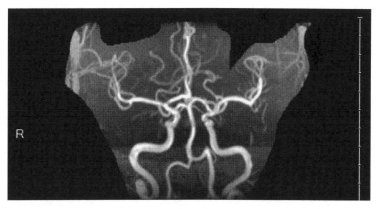

Pictured above: For comparison, a more typical MRA result where both MCAs are fully developed and without blockages. Note the symmetry between the two hemispheres.

Chapter Thirty-One
Fathers and Sons

For a long time, I had questioned the meaning of my near-death experience. *Why was I saved while others in similar situations perished? What was God's plan for me?* The best explanation was simple and came from my good friend, Dave, a devout Christian. He told me that I may never know the reason why God chose to keep me in this world, but his best guess was that I was saved for the benefit of others. That, in some way, my living would make a positive difference in someone else's life. I find great comfort in Dave's answer and pray that there is some truth behind it. At the end of the day, we are all just instruments of God's love, and we should judge our lives by the positive differences we make for others.

****

Two years ago on a February evening, I received a phone call from my father who still resided in Florida. He proceeded to tell me that he had fallen trying to unplug a drain and had hit his head. He was calling me from the hospital where he had been admitted. From the sound in his voice I could tell he was weak and distraught. He was 85 years old, but in pretty good health. I flew down the next day, followed by my two brothers. We were told by his attending nephrologist that his kidneys were failing him and there was nothing that could be done to reverse the damage. The hospital suggested our father be admitted to hospice to die peacefully. Although it was a difficult decision, my brothers and I agreed.

My father wasn't the most spiritual of men. When I was a boy he attended church normally on Christmas, sometimes Easter as well. Since my mother had passed twelve years before, the only time that I know he attended church was the wedding ceremony of my daughter Taryn. He rarely spoke of his faith, but he was with me in the hospital after my surgery and listened intently as I recounted my visit to Heaven. As I watched my father grow weaker and weaker throughout his hospice stay, I held his hand and reminded him of my heavenly experience, assuring him that he truly was going to a better place. One day, the hospice chaplain came in and asked my father if he could pray with him. I didn't expect Dad to respond as he hadn't had the energy to speak for days, but I watched in amazement as my father turned his gaze towards the chaplain and, clear as a bell, replied, "Yes." My father passed away at 1:30 the following afternoon, and I like to believe that he accepted God and was completely at peace when he left this world.

And it shall come to pass that whosoever who calls upon the name of the Lord shall be saved. ~ *Acts 2:21 KJV*

I recalled my friend Dave's words about my life possibly being spared for the benefit of others, and I sincerely hope that my father took some small comfort in my faith in God and my experience with Heaven prior to his death.

After my father's passing in March of 2014, I shifted my attention towards helping my son, who had entered the financial securities industry a year or two earlier. While I was at Morgan Stanley, I had always dreamed of working with one, or all, of my children when they grew up. I thought it would have been a joy to work in a real family business, side by side with my children on an everyday basis. After graduating college, Tyler was offered a position as a financial adviser in a city close to our home. I was immensely proud of my son and wanted to work alongside him despite my disability. I had no authority to offer him a helping hand, just my advice and suggestions.

I decided for the sake of my son to try and retake the certification exams myself to regain my financial license. That way when Tyler met with prospective clients he could tell them that he had discussions with his father, a former Senior Vice President of Investments and a licensed financial investor. My loose advisory association with my son would lend credibility without requiring much of me.

I simply wanted to obtain my Series 7 and Series 66 licenses to make my son proud of me again. I applied to take the exams with a few minor modifications due to my disability status. The governing body for the financial industry allowed me to use a reader/recorder to help me read the questions and mark down the answers as needed. Also, I was allowed triple the allotted time to take the exam, twenty-one hours instead of seven due to my cognitive delay. With the help of the wonderful lady who read the questions to me when my eyes got tired, I was able to pass both exams, one on my first try, the other on my second attempt. Despite obtaining my licenses, I wasn't reneging on my word to my wife. Although it took me a long time, I recognized and came to accept that I wasn't mentally or physically capable of handling the daily tasks of a financial adviser that were now part of my son's job. But I could still make a good sounding board for my son. Now when Tyler calls me and asks for my advice, I can give it to him, not only as his father, but as a professionally licensed, albeit retired and disabled, financial adviser.

Chapter Thirty-Two
A New Hope

One night, the topic of my health came up while Louann and I were out to dinner with Mike and Caroline. Unbeknownst to my family, I had been having regular episodes of stroke-like symptoms for the past few months. The episodes didn't last long, maybe half an hour, but when they occurred, the entire right side of my face would become numb and droopy. Most of the doctors I'd encountered were not interested in any attempts to prolong my life. They all seemed grateful that I had even survived in the first place, entirely content to let me finish out my borrowed time without any further intervention.

While out to dinner with Dr. Mike and his wife, Louann casually mentioned the fleeting episodes of facial drooping. Mike said, "What you're describing is a TIA, a mini-stroke. It's essentially your body's way of warning you that a bigger stroke is coming. You can't just ignore something like that. I think it might be a good idea for you to get a second opinion about your blocked artery. Let me see what I can do."

Mike made some calls the following week and put me in contact with the highly rated neurosurgical department of a large hospital in Philadelphia. Before long, I had an appointment to see if anything could be done regarding the blockage in my left middle cerebral artery.

Louann and I drove to Philadelphia to meet with Dr. Jones in April. Of all the neurologists and neurosurgeons I'd met over the years, Dr. Jones was the first female, which immediately earned her my respect. I imagine it's not easy to thrive in an alpha-male-dominated subspecialty like neurosurgery. Her success in her field showed me right away that she was doggedly persistent, tough, and incredibly motivated. I admired those qualities in any individual, and I was excited by the prospect of her agreeing to work with me.

On our first visit, she thoroughly reviewed all of my previous medical records and imaging studies from earlier hospitalizations and ordered a few more tests of her own. First up was a CT perfusion study, which uses a special dye and rapidly timed interval scans to assess and map out the specific areas of my brain that are at risk for decreased blood flow and stroke. With this test, we could watch in real time how much blood was getting to each part of my brain and which areas were not receiving as much blood as they should be. We already knew that I had the 100 percent MCA blockage on the left and the 50 percent MCA stenosis on the right, but this test could show us exactly how much these abnormalities were affecting the blood flow to the rest of my brain.

The results of the perfusion study came back pretty quickly but, unfortunately, they weren't exactly what Dr. Jones and I had been hoping for. We were hoping that things had stayed relatively stable and that the collateral arteries that had formed around my blocked left MCA were still providing enough blood flow to keep me alive and functioning. However, over the three years that had passed since my last scan, the collaterals were beginning to fail, which explained why I kept experiencing those symptoms on my right side. Dr. Jones informed us that over one-third of the collateral vessels had deteriorated, not functioning as well as a few years prior. *I was basically a ticking time bomb, a massive stroke just waiting to happen.*

"What can we do? I see his symptoms getting worse, even though he tries to hide them from me." Louann asked, looking first at Dr. Jones and then her eyes coming back to find mine. "At this point, I don't think surgery is an option. Try to avoid stress and stay well hydrated. Enjoy your life." Dr. Jones replied.

Receiving news of this nature was nothing new for Louann and me, but that didn't make it hurt any less. Over the years, I'd been told plenty of times that I'd been living on borrowed time, but perhaps my hourglass was finally running out of sand.

Spring turned into summer and my mini-stroke episodes persisted. I wasn't entirely sure if I was supposed to seek treatment for these episodes; every online resource I consulted told me that I should go to the emergency room, but I had gone there for this once, and they monitored me for a few hours and then sent me home without any answers. It just felt like a waste of time.

Whenever I'd feel symptoms coming on, I'd do my best to make sure my family didn't witness it. I knew they'd force me to go to the ER to be seen, and I saw no point in it anymore. There was nothing anyone could do; it was all just a big waiting game. Even though I tried not to think about it, the threat of something bad happening loomed in the back of my mind. As the upsetting thoughts pervaded into my consciousness, I immediately recognized that I had to shut them down and refocus myself on the full appreciation of the present moment. I frankly didn't have enough time left to waste any of it worrying over medical prognostications regarding my future. I needed to live my life and enjoy the time I had left. My remaining time on this earth should not be spent ruminating on the inevitabilities of my fate; it should be spent doing things that I love with the people that I love.

It was during an August picnic at our house that my secret episodes would be displayed for the entire family. All at once, I started to feel a distinct tingle on the right side of my face. *Oh no.... not now. Not in front of everyone, please.* Terror overtook me; I knew an episode was imminent, and it was going to happen in front of nearly every single person that I cared about. I tried to hide my face by looking off into the distance, hoping no one would notice how much the right side of my mouth had started to droop. I avoided all conversation, desperately wanting to get up and walk away, but unsure if I'd be able to stand up without stumbling or falling. The very last thing I wanted was to fall and make a scene. *You're safer just sitting here, Dale. Act normal. Just get through the next twenty minutes, and they won't know.*

"Dad?" Tristin somehow picked up on the subtle change in my demeanor instantly, "Is everything okay?"

"Yeah honey, I'm fine." The words slurred as they left my lips, exposing the exact deficit that I had been hoping to hide. I knew these symptoms were only temporary, but Tristin was going to panic if she saw me like this.

"Dad," she repeated, walking closer, "Dad, look at me."

I reluctantly turned towards her and grinned weakly, the right side of my face not even making an effort to cooperate with the left.

"That's it…MOM!!!" Tristin yelled, "Dad's having his face thing again. We need to take him to the hospital."

My skin became flushed as all of my party guests turned their attention towards examining the right half of my face.

"Tris, seriously, it's not a big deal. It'll be over in a few minutes. By the time we get to the hospital, there will be nothing to even examine. Just drop it, please. Let's get back to the picnic."

"Seriously Dad, you really don't look good," my other daughter Taryn chimed in as others nodded their heads in agreement.

"When did it get this bad?" my daughter-in-law Gina asked. "Louann said you got tingly on occasion, but she didn't mention anything like this. This is a legit transient ischemic attack, a TIA. How often has this been happening?"

Gina is a physician assistant and often gets stuck fielding all of our family's medical questions. *Apparently, Lou told her about my mini-strokes now, too.*

"Look guys, I'm not going to the ER right now," I announced firmly. "I appreciate everyone's concern, but there is nothing they can do for me there; I just have to ride it out. I promise if my face still looks like this in an hour or two, then we can talk about going and getting it checked out, okay? Now can we please go back to enjoying the day?"

No one was particularly pleased with me after I stubbornly refused to seek medical treatment but, as expected, my symptoms slowly resolved over the next half hour, and I returned back to normal. I tried my best to enjoy the rest of the afternoon, but the entire tone of the party was irreparably impacted by the awkwardness of my mini-stroke episode.

The very next day, Tristin took it upon herself to call Dr. Jones' office to describe what had happened to me at the party. Without my knowledge, she booked another appointment for me during which Dr. Jones scheduled me for another CT perfusion study and a different test that I'd never had before: a cerebral angiogram.

The perfusion study came back slightly worse than the one only four months prior. My collaterals were continuing to deteriorate. *It seemed like it was only a matter of time now; my decline was imminent.* The cerebral angiogram was scheduled for a few weeks later, and it would take place in the hospital. From what I'd learned, the angiogram was a more invasive procedure than ones I'd previously undergone. It required that I first be sedated under anesthesia, and then Dr. Jones would insert a thin flexible catheter into an artery near my groin and thread the catheter up through my blood vessels until it got near my brain. From there, she could use contrast material and imaging to get the most detailed view of what my arteries truly looked like.

During her research, Dr. Jones discovered that there may be a procedure she could try on me to help revascularize my brain. It was called an encephalo-duro-arterio-synangiosis (EDAS) procedure, and it was originally developed to treat patients who had developed Moyamoya disease, a rare vascular disorder that caused cerebral blood vessels to narrow and close off resulting in decreased blood flow to parts of the brain. While I didn't specifically have

Moyamoya disease, my condition had some parallels, and Dr. Jones believed that the procedure could greatly benefit my condition. The only requirement was that my cerebral vessels needed to be in good shape to tolerate the procedure as it was typically performed on a younger subset of patients. She had hoped that since I was a previously well-conditioned athlete who never smoked or drank, I might have blood vessels healthy enough to tolerate the procedure. The cerebral angiogram was going to be the true test. *Was I fixable?*

The day of the procedure, I dealt with the usual nervousness, but Louann remained with me every step of the way. As I lay in the hospital bed after the procedure, slowly awakening from the fog of the anesthesia, I felt a familiar tingle spread across the right side of my face. *Oh come on, you have got to be kidding me. Again? Now?* Dr. Jones immediately appeared at my bedside and informed me that she was admitting me overnight for observation. I tried to argue with her, but she abruptly stonewalled me, "Look, Mr. Reppert, I'm your neurosurgeon, and I just watched you have a TIA. If you think that I'm letting you go home after witnessing that, you're crazy. Now, stop arguing with me. You're going upstairs."

A few hours later, Dr. Jones returned to join my wife and me upstairs in my hospital room. "Ok, so Mr. Reppert, the bad news is that you had a small transient ischemic event during the procedure and, yes, that's unfortunate, but do you want to hear the good news?"

Louann leaned in, eyes widened in surprise. It had been a while since someone had told her there was some good news regarding my condition, "There's good news?" she remarked.

"Yes, there is. Your arteries look great. If you're still up for it, I'd be willing to attempt the revascularization procedure. I think you could tolerate it, but not without some risk."

I was stunned. *I had just had another mini-stroke on the table during a minor procedure. Was I really healthy enough to tolerate a brain surgery?*

"Now, in my opinion, time is of the essence," she continued. "The mini-strokes are happening more often, and the perfusion studies are showing that your cerebral blood flow is continuing to decline. I'd like to schedule the procedure ten days from today. I'd prefer to do it tomorrow if I could, but we need to wait at least ten days to get you off your blood-thinners first. I think that, if we're going to do this, it needs to be done as soon as possible."

"Thank you Dr. Jones. Would I be able to have some time to discuss things with my wife before I give you an official answer?"

"Absolutely! Take all the time you need. Please feel free to call my office if you have any questions or concerns."

I was discharged from the hospital the next day and took a full week to discuss the idea of surgery with Louann before our next visit with Dr. Jones. Without the surgery, it was only a matter of time before my remaining collaterals died off and led to a potentially massive stroke that would either paralyze or kill me. The surgery at least gave me the possibility of an extended life expectancy; it provided optimism when none had existed months before.

As crazy as it sounds, one of my wife's and my biggest concerns regarding the surgery was that we'd already planned (and paid for) two vacations in celebration of our 36th wedding anniversary. We had intended to spend a week in a small cabin in the mountains of Gatlinburg, Tennessee in September and then had even bigger plans to take the entire family to Disney World the next month. After the news in April, we decided to have our summer of fun, culminating with these two trips. I had been so excited for both trips that I couldn't imagine postponing them. My two grandchildren had never been to Disney, and I had been looking forward to this trip ever since my oldest granddaughter, Vivienne, was born. *How could I miss this opportunity? What if I cancelled the trips, went through with the surgery, and then died on the table? I'd never get to see my grandkids experience Disney World.* My previous luck with brain surgeries was pretty poor to say the least; I couldn't risk a bad outcome.

My wife said "Dr. Jones, we are leaving in a few days for an anniversary trip followed by a family reunion to Disney World shortly after that." Dr. Jones replied, "I understand. Definitely take your trips because there is risk with the surgery. Enjoy your time, Dale. Please let me know if you want to schedule the procedure after getting back from your trip. We can schedule it as soon as you return."

Thankful for caring physicians, I headed home from Philadelphia that evening determined to enjoy both of my vacations and praying for God's guidance regarding the path that I should take.

Chapter Thirty-Three
A Balanced Life and Family

It has been said many times that "Hindsight is 20/20" and this is true not only in finance, but in life. Financially, an investor could always look back into the past and see what trades should or shouldn't have been made with perfect clarity. *I mean, it's easy to know the right move to make after the outcome has been determined, but it's a bit harder to make those moves ahead of time.* Life is no different. As I felt my life slipping away in that hospital bed, I looked back upon my time on earth and couldn't help thinking about all the things I should have done.

Now that's not to say that I was completely wrong for working hard and trying to be successful in my career, but perhaps I devoted too much time to that specific aspect of my life at the expense of other important parts of my life. Throughout my ordeal, I've come to realize that true happiness requires a healthy state of balance based upon three underlying types of wealth: financial, spiritual, and experiences/memories. Prior to becoming sick, my life was truly unbalanced; the financial pursuit of the wealth dimension of my life took priority over everything including my family and my faith. I missed out on a lot of things, special moments in my children's lives that I can't get back no matter how much I want to. I missed out on quality time with my wife, opportunities to tell her how much she means to me, how amazing she is as a mother, and how I still see her through the eyes of a love-struck twenty-one year old. I neglected my faith, missing chances to develop and strengthen my relationship with God. My second chance allowed me the opportunity to become whole again, to cultivate all dimensions of my life equally and to appreciate the joy that comes through balance. While I hate that it took a near-death experience for me to come to this realization, I am so incredibly thankful that I have been given this second chance.

It was a month after our visit to Dr. Jones that Louann and I celebrated our thirty-sixth wedding anniversary in Florida at Walt Disney World with our entire family. This vacation was unlike any other for me personally. Past family vacations to Disney were often interrupted by visits to the local Morgan Stanley office, countless calls from pay phones to check in with clients, and hours spent left behind at the hotel catching up on paperwork while my children explored the parks with my wife. Even when I was able to accompany my family to the parks, my thoughts were constantly consumed with work, and I never truly enjoyed the moment or appreciated the magic of Disney World. *I wouldn't make that mistake this time.*

The scheduling of the vacation worked out so well that all three of my children, both sons-in-law, my daughter-in-law, and my two grandchildren were all able to be there to help Lou and I celebrate. We went on rides, met Disney characters, shared indulgent dinners, and reminisced about the good times of the past.

We ate entirely too much, exercised way too little, and laughed to the point of tears on multiple occasions. I was fortunate enough to witness my three year-old granddaughter Vivienne experience the parks for the very first time. Ever since she was born, I'd been looking forward to taking her to Disney World, hoping to recapture some of the joy from when my own children were little. Just as I'd hoped, Vivi's eyes lit up at the splendor of Cinderella's Castle and as she bravely rode her first ride with me beside her. She giggled the entire time and shouted, "Again! Again!" as we stepped out of the cart. She pointed at every toy she walked past in the gift shop, "I'd like this one please, GranDale. Ooh no, wait, this one, this one!" She knew she had me wrapped around her finger, and I fought the urge to buy her every single toy she desired, not wanting to spoil her too much or bankrupt myself in the process. Despite my restraint, she still received her share of souvenirs, carefully chosen from the plethora of stuffed animals and figurines.

Being at the parks with Vivi was fantastic, but surprisingly, my favorite memory of the trip took place in the hotel pool. Vivi and I laughed and swam together for nearly two hours, taking turns pretending to be sharks and sea creatures. When she wanted to catch me, she'd tell me that I was a turtle and I could only move in super slow motion until she caught up with me. When I got to be the shark, I'd ominously hum the "Jaws" theme song every time I resurfaced from under the water, the song becoming louder and faster the closer I came to her. She squealed and giggled with delight as I lifted her high up into the air, "I got you! Ahhh!" My mind flickered back to similar situations when my own children were young, and I desperately wished that I had taken the time to

151

be truly present and to have created more of these precious memories with them.

Seeing all of my children together, grown up and with families of their own, was nothing short of a dream come true. Our last night, as I stood in the middle of the Magic Kingdom awaiting the fireworks, I purposefully took in the view of my family surrounding me: Taryn and her husband Jerry playfully laughing with one another, Tristin, my cute grandson William nestled in her arms, her husband Bill with my sweet Vivi perched happily upon his shoulders, Tyler and his wife Gina, her head resting peacefully on his chest. I slung my arms around my wife's shoulders and whispered in her ear, "Look at our beautiful family, Lou. Could there ever be anything better than this?" And then, as if straight out of a movie, fireworks began to light up the night sky.

Chapter Thirty-Four
Louann: Still Dale

Twelve years ago, I could not have foreseen the journey that awaited my husband after his diagnosis of a Chiari malformation and the new normal which would dictate our life today. From the outside looking in, we're still just your average couple. We go to the movies regularly, play tennis together, hunt for sales at the outlet malls, and share time together. We enjoy hanging out with our friends and, lately, over the past couple of years, we've planned weddings and showers for all three of our children. To the casual observer, things may look perfectly normal, but I know that they're not.

My husband has fought extremely hard to get back to where he is today, and he's come a long way from the depleted condition the meningitis and sepsis had left him in. A good amount of his progress was made because of denials. He consistently denied his limitations and did his best to ignore his pain whenever possible. He still does. In addition, Dale has learned to deal with his shortcomings by utilizing humor, often making light of his inadequacies. Previously, it would have bothered him when he couldn't remember what he ordered off the menu at dinner, but now he laughs when his surprise meal arrives. Although his habit of minimizing his problems can be truly frustrating at times, my husband's courage and persistence simply cannot be denied.

Our family has grown closer together since my husband's illness, and Dale has returned to being the father and husband he once was, still possessing the same love and concern he's always had for his family. Our family has also healed together, our temporary scars slowly mending with time. That's not to say that Dale still has the same intuitive and seamless connections with us as he once had. His reactions are slower due to his eye and vestibular issues, and he still zones out when he is tired or stressed. *But he's still Dale.*

Actually, he's a better person now. He is kinder, more empathetic, softer, and more patient. He appreciates things about the world around him now that he never even used to notice; he loves deeper, forgives quicker, and chooses to give others the benefit of the doubt. Dale consistently looks for ways to give back to others and has made it his mission to help others. While my husband's illness took a lot from him, I believe he has received more blessings than losses as a result.

Chapter Thirty-Five
Measuring Wealth

Over the years, a handful of people have approached me to ask about the ways I've changed as a result of the brief moments I got to spend in Heaven. Although I may have only been there for a short time, the experience was enough to transform my entire worldview.

How many times have you heard someone tell you to "stop and smell the roses"? In my lifetime, I must have heard that phrase hundreds of times, yet I never really gave it much thought prior to my battle with meningitis. Before my illness, I would wake up in the morning and immediately flip on the financial news to begin my workday. My career was the driving force behind most days, and I made very little time for life's quiet moments, quite frankly assuming that there were better, much more productive ways in which I could spend my time.

Since my life's detour, many things have changed regarding how I perceive the world around me and how I value each moment. Every day since my illness, I've awoken with a sense of gratitude, knowing that I was not owed this day, yet thankful that it has been given to me. When I began to recognize that each day was a gift,

I started to enjoy the beauty in the little things that so often went overlooked. I found joy in bird watching, partaking in early morning strolls with my wife, and watching sunsets. I began catching up with old friends again, spending time laughing and recounting old memories. I marveled at my grandchildren and how their curious minds discover more and more about the world around them each day.

As a result of my journey, I have been awakened to the joys of a simple life unburdened by the meaningless pursuit of wealth or status. My self-worth no longer hinges on my job title or my professional success but rather is built purposefully day by day from the kindness and generosity that I receive and try to give. My eyes have finally been opened to the moments and the things that truly matter and, despite my disability, I feel happier and more fulfilled now than I ever did before.

While I may no longer be wealthy in the usual sense of the word, the years that I have been unable to work have provided me with a surplus of the world's most precious currency — time. I have been given countless hours with my family that I never would have gotten to experience had I continued my career at Morgan Stanley. Of course, there are some things that I am incapable of doing now, things that I used to excel at, but God's detour has allowed me a whole new perspective on life. I've learned that time is the one commodity that we cannot get back and that the way in which we choose to spend that time dictates our happiness.

One can choose to chase things that may seem important at the time, like money, status, or fame, but as life draws to a close,

I've found that none of that stuff really matters much. The wealthiest of us at death are those that have the fondest memories of life.

Postscript

As for me, I finally came to a decision regarding the recommended brain surgery after returning to my hotel room, granddaughter in tow. I owed it to my wife, family and grandchildren to agree to the surgery.

Reppert family photo from 2014 at my son Tyler's wedding

Epilogue
Tristin: Dad's Third Brain Surgery

My father scheduled his third brain surgery for December 1, 2016. The news that he agreed to have the EDAS procedure done was thrilling and crushing at the same time. Without the surgery, I realized he may not be around in a year to give me fatherly advice and that my daughter Vivienne could lose her favorite person. While I'm a self-proclaimed Daddy's girl, Vivi is GranDale's girl. Watching my father interact with my daughter is a blessing I never take for granted. The thought of never seeing my dad blow Vivienne silly tiger kisses at bedtime or play pretend games of superhero with her caused an unbearable pain I had never experienced before.

The week leading up to his surgery I vacillated between hope and despair. I had witnessed my dad's struggles since his first procedure to correct his Chiari malformation and knew how strong he was, but was he strong enough to undergo a third brain surgery? I knew the surgery held great risk for my father and I was petrified we would lose him on the operating table.

I prayed alongside family and friends the day of his surgery as we placed our trust in God and his neurosurgeon. After four hours in the operating room, I received a call from my mom that

Dad was stable and in the ICU recovering. I cried tears of joy and thought, "God is good."

Acknowledgements

We wish to thank God foremost, our families, and our friends; Taryn, Tristin, and Tyler, thank you for making our family complete and always supporting us. Mike and Caroline who we consider to be our earthly angels. Paul and Kim, who have been with us from the beginning of our eventful journey. Dave and Patty, who encouraged us to share our story. Andy and Bill and Linda and Basil, whose friendship kept us going. Gary and Vicky, Barry and Diane, and Steve and Laurie who supported us with love and compassion. Donna, who has been our lifelong friend. The tennis guys, Al, Oscar, John, and Tom who brought hope and joy back in the form of tennis. Our photographer, Jacquelyn Kolosow, who provided the beautiful cover photo. Vault Collective, for designing our wonderful book jacket. Casey Styons and Janet Reppert for proofreading. And a big thank you to Elizabeth Gibney Woytovitch for her editing services.

About the Author

Dale Reppert currently resides in Kutztown, PA. Far removed from his old life as a Sr. VP at a major financial firm, he enjoys spending time with his wife, three children, and two grandchildren. He finds joy in tennis, a good movie, and practicing his faith. Dale is currently recovering from his third brain surgery and looking forward to what the future holds, as well as continuing to share his heavenly experience with others.

Thank you for reading.
We invite you to share your thoughts.

info@detourtoheaven.com

http://www.detourtoheaven.com

https://www.facebook.com/Detourtoheaven

Made in the USA
Columbia, SC
25 May 2018